Mac

Macmillan Professional Masters

Titles in the series

Supervision

Mike Savedra
and
John Hawthorn

MACMILLAN

First published by Pan Books Ltd in 1984 as
Supervision: a fresh approach in the Breakthrough series.

Fully updated and revised edition published in 1990 by
MACMILLAN EDUCATION LTD
Houndmills, Basingstoke, Hampshire RG21 2XS
and London
Companies and representatives
throughout the world

Printed in Hong Kong

British Library Cataloguing-in-Publication Data
Savedra, Mike
Supervision.
1. Management. Supervision—Manuals
I. Title II. Hawthorn, John
658.3'02
ISBN 0–333–51546–3
ISBN 0–333–51547–1 Pbk
ISBN 0–333–51548–X Pbk export

Contents

List of Illustrations

1 Getting Started

1.1 Introduction

This book is about the work and problems of supervisors in all types of jobs. We aim to help you to improve your supervisory performance, and believe that the book will be of value to potential supervisors and managers at all levels.

The job of the supervisor is a difficult one. In the simplest terms supervisors have to get things done, achieve results, and get the work completed to the requirements of their managers. Your job is to get things done through people, to organise staff and resources to achieve results, and to make sure that everything is running smoothly. We explore the work of the supervisor more fully in Chapter 2.

The format of the book
The book is designed to help the process of *self-study*. Throughout you will find questions which you are encouraged to answer before reading any further. There are three types of question:

Self-checks: these are usually short questions or tasks requiring quick answers designed to help you check on your own learning. Answers are given directly after the self-check. Try to answer the question before reading on and please read our answer before moving on to the next topic. You can read on without attempting the questions, but you will be missing a chance to learn. In many cases our answers enlarge on the subject.

Activities: these usually ask you to use some information which you will not find in the text. To answer these questions you have to use your own experience or discover some fresh facts for yourself. Sometimes an activity is simply an opportunity for you to stop and think about an important point raised in the text.

Exercises: these test your understanding of something that has been explained. They ask you to carry out some task, and you can then check your responses by looking at the answers at the back of the book.

Acknowledgements
Many people have contributed to the ideas that are outlined in this book. Above all it is supervisors like you that we have learnt from and tested our ideas against. Some of the supervisors that we know will appear later in the book; we hope that you can learn from their problems. Next there are the originators of the ideas that we have used and tested, the writers

of books and the researchers. We have taken ideas from wherever we have found them.

The shape of the book
This is a book that you can pick and choose from. You do not have to read it from beginning to end; you can choose sections that interest you. Only you know what you need.

The book is laid out as follows:

* In this chapter we will help you to decide what sort of *learning* you need and how to exercise the basic skills of *studying*.
* In Chapter 2 we will examine the *work of the supervisor* and describe a general picture of supervisory work which will help you to choose which parts of the book are likely to be most valuable to you.
* Chapter 3–8 are related to *various aspects of the supervisor's work*, and you can choose from these to suit your needs.
* Chapter 9 draws the threads together and shows how they all fit into the work of the average supervisor.

1.2 **What You Need**

This book is intended for readers in four categories:
* Supervisors who want to improve their performance on their own.
* Readers who are following a NEBSM or ISM course in supervisory management.
* Managers who want to help their supervisors to improve their performance.
* Students who are following a course which includes management subjects.

Whichever category of reader you are, the very fact that you are reading this book now means that you are already well on the way with the process of learning to improve your performance. You have made a start, and this book can help you to carry the process on. But first we have to look at learning itself.

You have been learning since the day you were born, so why make an issue of it now? Here are four reasons:

* Learning can be particularly effective if it is done in a *systematic way*.
* Supervisors are often people who think themselves unsuited to 'book learning' and need guidance on how to *use a book effectively*.
* A lot of the work of supervisors is concerned with training their staff, so they are concerned with *other people's learning*.

- Many people just take their job for granted and learn nothing constructive from their *daily experiences*.

The rest of this chapter helps you to decide what you need to learn about supervisory management, and how to use the book to maximum effect.

1.3 What Style of Learning Suits you Best?

This book can help you with your learning, but it cannot make you learn anything. The responsibility for your learning rests with you. People are individuals and learn in different ways. It is therefore important that you are clear about yourself – what sort of person are you? How do you learn best?

Are you careful, thoughtful in your decisions, or are you hasty and impatient and eager to step in and get things done? Do you want to know how things work, the theory behind the fact, or is it the challenge of something new that makes you get stuck in?

Activity

How would you answer? In five minutes, write as much as you can about yourself.

It is important for you to think this through because:

- You are an *individual*.
- You learn best in *your own way*.
- You need to identify the way in which you have *previously learned*.
- You should try to evaluate *other ways of learning*.

If you are hasty, eager to get results, you will probably try anything once – this approach to life will be reflected in your enthusiastic, open-minded approach to learning. Try out new ideas, experiment for yourself, develop your own style.

Thoughtful people learn differently, they collect data from many sources, chew things over, sort it out for themselves, and then act. *Analysis* and *evaluation* are high on their list of learning priorities. If this is your style, you may take longer to try something out, but when you do you will have it all together.

Theorists enjoy the complex but logical theories behind actions they encounter. As a consequence they reject ideas that do not fit their understanding. If this is your style, draw your own theories from the ideas that we present.

People who enjoy challenge are mainly concerned with making things work – getting on with it is what drives them. To you we say, do get on with it, but look at the implications for *other people*; you need people to make things happen.

Activity

What was the last thing you learned? Close the book and cast your mind back over recent events; was there a significant learning point that may affect your approach to your work in the future? (Five minutes.)

The answer to this question will be very much a personal thing. Here are some answers from a group of supervisors:

- 'I saw a guy in a television programme giving orders to someone and thought that there was no way that he'd get the job done – makes you think . . . '
- 'My son's got a small computer and he showed me a fabulous program that can make my job so much easier, I'm trying to convince my boss.'
- 'I had a new job to do and I tried out this new way. My boss thought it wouldn't work but it did – now we use it all the time.'

1.4 **Levels of Learning**

Everybody learns in different ways, and there is an ascending scale of effectiveness in the ways that you use your learning opportunities.

- You can *copy* exactly what other people do (this is how children start to learn), or do exactly what you are told.
- You can observe what other people do, *analyse* their successes and failures and, once you understand what is going on, *transfer* the useful ideas to your own work.
- You can *evaluate* your own experience and then apply your own ideas from what you have learned.
- You can deliberately test situations by asking 'what would happen if?' and then *experimenting* with your own work.

Introducing Tom Stranks
Look at the story of Tom Stranks and what happened to him the other day. We will be referring to Tom's experiences in other chapters.

People Under Pressure

Tom, the section leader of A line, was having one of those days. Four of his girls were away sick, leaving him with only twenty operators of which two were trainees. Production was slow, there was a shortage of some components and those produced in other departments were often not up to the required quality standards. Instead of returning these faulty components Tom was rectifying them on his section as this saved both time and paperwork.

On top of this, the recently installed machines were producing only at 80 per cent of their normal rate. Tom was examining these machines when Bill Betts, the works manager, sent for him.

'Come in, Tom – missed you at the special production meeting this morning', he said.

'Sorry, chief, I forgot all about it, I've got a load of problems on A line and – '

'Forget A line for now,' interrupted Bill. 'You should have been at the meeting. Anyway I've got a new job for you for the next four days. D line has had two days' output rejected by Inspection and Tony is being awkward about the rectifications required. I haven't got time to argue with him as I'm away in Manchester for the next two days so I'm putting you in charge. Just sort it out. OK?'

Tom had a thousand questions to ask but Bill was already preparing to leave, so he said as firmly as he could:

'Bill, you know that nobody knows anything about D line, it's a closed book to most people. Anyway my own section's in trouble – I've got four girls away this morning and . . . '

'That reminds me,' said Bill. 'I've asked the B and C section leaders to let you have anyone that they can spare so you should have four or five people to help you on this job. I know Tony should sort this out but he's always been touchy about having the highest reject rate in the company and anyway you know the product inside out. I haven't got the time to argue with him, so get this lot sorted out as quick as you can – you'll soon pick it up.' And with that he left.

Self-check

What does this incident show? What could you learn from it if you were Tom? (Fifteen minutes.)

This sort of incident occurs when people are under pressure. The manager is pressing Tom because he is under pressure himself. Tom has to cope with this at the time, but when things settle down he can reconsider these events and talk things through with his manager.

Tom should:

- consider whether this sort of treatment from his manager is *acceptable*;
- check his *objectives* and *areas of responsibility*;
- get his *priorities* clear and be prepared to *negotiate* for them;
- *question things*.

If you have experiences like this you can *learn from them*.
The areas open to you for learning come from three main sources:

- Your *own experience*.
- *Advice from other people*, which is the distillation of their experience.
- *Other sources* like newspapers, journals, books and television.

Everything you learn can be seen as either skills or knowledge. Knowledge is facts, ideas, concepts and you can learn these quite quickly, although it is of little or no use to you if you do not understand them. Skills are more difficult to learn because they are concerned with applications, and to become skilful you have to practise. For example, you could learn all the facts about the working parts of a bicycle, but that would be of little use to you if you wanted to learn how to ride it: you have to practise.

To help you learn from this book we are going to explain briefly how to practise some of the skills that you will use.

How to use a book
Read a book as you would read a newspaper – read only the parts *that you need*. Using a book properly should involve several stages:

- *Survey*: each book has a *structure* which is outlined in the contents at the start of the book. Look through this to find out what it can offer.
- *Question*: what do *you want* out of the book? Always approach a book with questions that you want answered.
- *Read, recall, review*: read the parts that *interest you*. Recall what you have read by pausing occasionally and telling yourself the main parts of what you have read. Review your work by checking to see if your questions have been answered.

Study Skills, by Kate Williamson, in the Macmillan Professional Masters series is an excellent guide to the ways in which you can improve your study skills.

Self-check

Did you survey *Supervision*? List the main headings. (Two minutes.)

Check your list against the contents page at the front of the book. How well does it compare?

How to make notes

Making notes is a skill which you will often need to use in your job as a supervisor. The essential skills are those of *listening* and those of *summarising*. To summarise effectively note the essential parts of the message and edit out all the other material. The note then gives you a written record of the events which you wish to recall.

Activity

Next time the radio broadcasts a weather forecast, be prepared, and make notes of the essential points as it is read. If you can, tape-record the broadcast, and then play it back to see how well you have summarised the essential facts. (Ten minutes.)

Solving problems, making decisions

An essential part of learning is *evaluating your experiences*. Thinking back over what has happened and working out why it happened is rather like solving problems. You solve problems and make decisions every day, but have you ever thought about *how you do it*? The process can be described as a step-by-step procedure which is worth following with care when you have a big decision to make.

- Define your aim – *what you are trying to achieve*. This can be stated in broad terms.
- *Collect the facts*.
- *List the choices*. Be careful not to let your thinking be limited at this step. Be creative. Even silly ideas should be listed when they come to you. They can be weeded out later.
- *Predict the outcomes*. Consider, for all the choices, how things might turn out. This will select the valuable possibilities.
- *Make the decision*.

Using a 'mentor'
If after all this you are keen to further your learning as a means of improving your performance and gaining more satisfaction from your work, then you might consider using a 'mentor'. This may sound rather heavy but all it means is finding someone to talk to about the things that you are trying to do.

Your mentor may be a friend at work, your wife, or someone you meet in the social club – it does not matter who, as long as you have someone to discuss things and test your views with. You want a person who will point out things to you that you do not recognise for yourself.

Learning from experience
Above all, the main thing is to become analytical, to look at everything with *an observer's eye*. The cycle of learning is:

? Something raises a question in your mind which causes you to *think* and formulate ideas of your own.

● Using these ideas you put them into practice and *act* on the results of your thoughts.

● As a result of your action something happens and you *reflect* on the outcome.

? This may raise *further questions*, and the cycle is started all over again.

Does it make *you* think?

2 Supervisory Management

In this chapter we will be discussing what supervisory management *is*, and how it differs from *other levels of management*. We will show that, although supervisors work in many different environments and in numerous industries, there are many common elements in the supervisory aspects of their work. The main supervisory duties will be identified, analysed and discussed, together with the skills needed for effective supervision.

Many supervisors whom we have met are women doing a first-rate job of running their sections; however, throughout the book, we have referred to the supervisor as 'he'. This is to avoid clumsy 'he/she', 'himself/herself' constructions: we hope that the use of 'he' as a general pronoun will not cause any offence to women supervisors.

You are an individual and *your needs are unique*. You will want to know how you can develop into a more effective supervisor. At the end of this chapter are a checklist and a questionnaire which will help you to do this.

The first of these list many of the tasks/duties that supervisors perform, and is useful in formally identifying the *sort of job you do*. The second list allows you to evaluate *how well you perform* these tasks that you have identified. This evaluation, together with the personal analysis that follows the lists, should provide you with the information you need to decide which section of the book you want to read, and possibly the order in which you wish to approach them.

You can either go directly to these lists now or deal with them once you have read through the chapter.

2.1 What Sort of Organisation do You Work in?

Jobs which can be labelled 'supervisor' are found in all sorts of organisations, and the examples of supervisory work that we quote show just a few of them. In this section, we will use 'organisation' to mean a group of people employed to achieve specific objectives. We will concentrate on organisations which employ people, and will ignore voluntary organisations like sports clubs and charities, which have their own special problems.

Activity

How many different types of organisation can you think of? List them and put them into different categories, such as large/small, for example. (Ten minutes.)

Some possible differences that you might have identified are:

- Large organisations/small organisations.
- Manufacturers/non-manufacturers.
- Public sector/private sector.
- Makers of simple products/makers of complex products.
- Profit-making/non-profit-making.

There are distinct differences between some of these organisations, and we need a summary which puts them into orderly groupings. One way is show in Figure 2.1.

Fig 2.1   *Types of organisation*

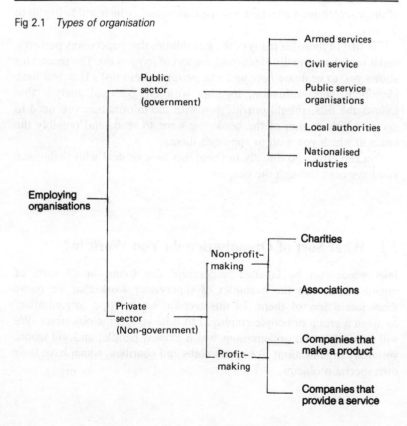

Consider the organisation that you work for. Which of these categories would you fit it into? The type of organisation and what it is trying to achieve will affect the *beliefs of the people in the organisation* and the *general working atmosphere* that exists. These factors add up to a sort of organisational 'climate' which can make working life pleasant in some cases and miserable in others.

2.2 What is the Organisation Trying to do?

All organisations exist *for a purpose*. They are trying to achieve something, as indicated by the list of types in Figure 2.1.

Activity

What are the objectives of your organisation? Write down what you think its objectives are, in simple terms. (Five minutes.)

It is easy to write 'to make profit' if you work in a private-sector company, but this is too vague because it hides so much. Profit is crucial to the survival of the company, because if it fails to make a profit over several years it will not survive; but profit is only an indicator, and the company makes a profit by *doing something else*, like making a range of products that customers want or by providing a service that meets people's needs. If you work for an organisation that does not have a profit motive then the objectives are more difficult to pin down; even within the organisation itself there may be no clear statement of objectives.

Someone who works for a further education college might define its objectives in this way: 'to provide a further education service for the locality in the most effective way, taking account of the educational needs of the students, the needs of employers, and the requirements of examining authorities'. Notice that there is no mention of profit, although the word 'effective' does mean that the college has to be cost-effective as well as meeting educational objectives.

The workings of the firm

All organisations, as we have seen, exist *for a purpose*, either to provide a service or to make a product. Money is an input to the organisation which it needs in order to marshal the resources which it must have to achieve its objectives. The private-sector company sells its products or services and thereby earns revenue which flows back into the business.

The public-sector organisation relies on grants from public money, which has been collected by means of rates or taxes; the grants are allocated largely from central government.

A diagram can be built up, as in Figures 2.2, 2.3 and 2.4, showing the main elements of money flow for a manufacturing company. First, we represent the plant where the manufacture is carried out, and the people who work there (Figure 2.2).

To show the manufacture, we represent it as a flow of materials which are purchased from suppliers, put through various processes and then assembled into a product to go out to the customers. This is added to the diagram as a material flow (Figure 2.3).

Fig 2.2 *Manufacturing company: main elements*

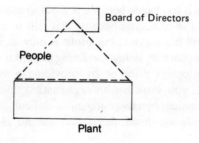

Fig 2.3 *Manufacturing company: material flow*

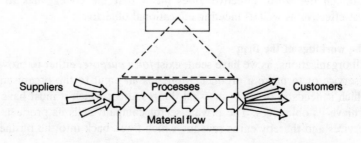

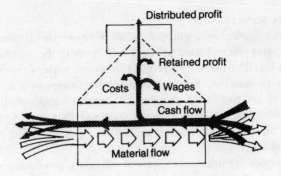

Fig 2.4 *Manufacturing company: money flow, material flow and profit*

Self-check

What is the other important flow in the manufacturing company? How can we best represent it? (Two minutes.)

The other flow is *cash*, which is the life-blood of the business. Money, cash, income, revenue, whatever you like to call it, flows back into the business as the goods are sold and is used to pay bills, pay the wages, cover the costs and provide profit for future developments. *Profit equals revenue less costs.* We can add this to the diagram, which finally looks like Figure 2.4.

If the material flow is held up, the goods do not get to the customer and the money does not flow back into the business. What the diagram does not show is the way in which supervisors can have an effect on the *control of costs*.

Self-check

How do supervisors have a part to play in the control of costs? (Five minutes.)

Every action generates a *cost*. The supervisor is in charge of a working group and this is a vital point where costs are incurred, so that the more cost-effective the section is the better. To understand this we need to look at the nature of the costs in a little more detail, and this is explored in Chapter 8 'Where does the superviser fit in?'.

Product or service?

The model shown in Figures 2.2–2.4 is based on a manufacturing company, and you will have to adapt it to apply to the organisation that you work for. The balance of product to service varies from one type of operation to another. For a manufacturing company the balance is heavily on *product*, with the service content much smaller. For a telephone company the objectives will be heavily geared to the *service* that they offer, with the product side of the business taking a relatively minor position.

For a service organisation the model still holds, given some changes of label. There will still be people working in the organisation, and they will be subject to direction from a senior management team. Money will flow into the business from its customers when they pay for the service that they receive. The material flow changes to information flow (like telephone calls flowing through the network of lines and exchanges) and the plant becomes whatever physical resources have to be set up to provide the service. In all cases, the organisation sets up a *structure*, to meet the objectives and satisfy the customers.

2.3 Features Affecting Organisational Climate

There are other features of your organisation which will affect the climate in it. Its size, age and rate of growth will be most important. Large and old organisations tend to create very strict levels – that is, there are many grades and ranks, often with set rules about status. If the rule book defines the size of the carpet in a manager's office according to his rank, for example, the organisation is likely to be large and old and will have many restrictive controls. Younger and smaller organisations will not be so set in their ways, but will expect people to exercise initiative when a problem arises, rather than automatically look in the rule book. Procedures will be much less clear and there will be a tendency to rely on *ad hoc* decisions.

Features of organisations

The parts of the organisation likely to affect your work are those *close to you*. The objectives and climate will be a permanent influence, but more immediate effects come from the relationships with those who work with you. The way you get on with your boss and the way you work with your staff are the most important factors in determining your job satisfaction. Around this unit of the organisation, the boss–supervisor–staff unit, certain features are true to all organisations. They start with the process by which work is shared around the organisation, the processs of *delegation* (see Figure 2.5).

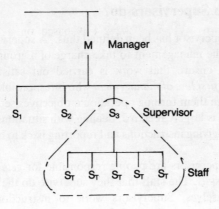

Fig 2.5   *The delegation process*

Delegation

If the workload of the manager increases to the point where he cannot do it all effectively, he has either to restrict his inputs of work or delegate part of it to a subordinate. Delegation is the process by which a manager decides that work he might otherwise do himself is passed on to a subordinate. This is the basis on which all organisations operate in some way or other.

Exercise 2.1

If manager M delegates task X to subordinate S3 (see Figure 2.5) and the task is properly explained, who is now responsible for that task? (Five minutes.)

2.4 Management

This leads us to look at the nature of managerial work in general. We can quote the words of a famous American, F. W. Taylor, who analysed his own experience and said: 'Management is getting things done through people.' So management work is concerned with achieving results by organising the efforts of others rather than by doing it yourself.

More precisely we can determine whether a position in an organisation is managerial by applying the definition of a later writer, Wilfred Brown, who wrote: 'A managerial role is one from which work is delegated to subordinate roles, the manager remaining accountable for the results'.

2.5   What do Supervisors do?

The job of the supervisor has been defined thus: 'A supervisor is a person selected by middle management to take charge of a group of people, or special task, to ensure that work is carried out satisfactorily'. The supervisor is the *first line of management* who is responsible for managing staff, and through them turning operational objectives set by others into actions. The job is largely reactive, dealing with situations as they arise, allocating work, giving instructions and reporting back to higher management.

In essence, supervisors are people responsible for *getting things done* and *achieving results*. The staff that they supervise do the work, they do not do it themselves. Supervisors work to instructions from their managers, using the procedures of the company, and achieve results by organising the efforts of the staff under their command.

The range of situations in which supervisors work is very wide.

Four supervisors' jobs

Terry, Pauline, Mark and Dave

- Terry is a supervisor in a factory. He supervises a section that assembles electrical components. He has 18 staff. 10 of these are skilled electricians, 6 are semi-skilled and 2 are unskilled – 1 labourer and 1 storeman. The hours of the section are regular 08.00 to 12 noon and 13.00 to 16.30 hours, five days a week. Some overtime is worked. Terry works to the schedule from Planning and concentrates on keeping the work going and solving problems.

- Pauline works for a nationwide retail chemists and supervises the photographic and audio section in one of their stores in the Thames Valley area. She has four staff, three of whom are part-time. The operating details of the section are laid down by detailed company procedures and most of the decisions are made by the manager of the store. Pauline's job is to allocate the work, make sure that the work is carried out properly and deal with any problems. She also has to do the paperwork that is necessary, recording work done, and ordering stock from the storeroom.

- Mark is a supervisor by the nature of his work, although not by his title. He is a senior operating department assistant and works in the operating theatre of a hospital in the National Health Service. Mark works as part of a team that includes surgeons, anaesthetists and nurses. Both routine and emergency work must be covered and there is the ever-present knowledge that mistakes could be fatal. He supervises two staff who are responsible for the technical functions of the operating theatre, getting it ready for the medical staff and ensuring that all the equipment is working satisfactorily. The section works to the operations schedule and to the hours necessary to complete it.

- Dave is a supervisor and is called by that title. He works in a local authority sports centre and supervises the work of six sports assistants who keep the centre clean, prepare facilities to requirements of the bookings and supervise the activities of the public who use the centre facilities such as the swimming pool. Since the centre is open for twelve hours on most days, Dave works on early or late shifts, as well as weekends. Dave exercises discipline and organisation over his staff but the atmosphere is informal.

2.6 Similarity of Supervisory Work

From this small sample of supervisory jobs you can see that supervisory work varies tremendously. Do not be confused by the details: concentrate on the broad picture, the similarities between Terry's, Pauline's, Mark's and Dave's jobs.

Exercise 2.2

Using these four examples, together with your own experience of supervisory management, list what you think are the common elements of all supervisory work. (Ten minutes.)

Supervisory tasks
We can now sum up and identify certain tasks that all supervisors perform:

- **Planning** Drawing up schedules to achieve targets that are set by either themselves or their bosses.
- **Organising** Arranging resources to enable the plan to be put into practice.
- **Motivating** Getting the best out of the staff involved.
- **Controlling** Comparing what is actually happening with the plan and taking any corrective action necessary.
- **Communicating** Telling those concerned what is going on, how they are doing, keeping in touch.
- **Problem solving** Coping with the day-to-day problems.
- **Decision making** Deciding on those areas that need personal attention.
- **Updating** Keeping up to date with safety and other types of legislation.

All these tasks are dealt with in later chapters in this book.

2.7   Differences in Supervisory Work

You have already identified that there are some common elements to all
supervisory work. There are also a great many differences between one
supervisory job and another.

Activity

Using the same four examples that you used in Exercise 2.2, together with
your own experience, list as many factors as you can that account for the
differences in supervision. (Ten minutes.)

You should have listed some or all of the following:

- The *technical content and complexity* of the job being supervised.
- The fact that some supervisors work *shifts* which will complicate the
  issue.
- The *number of staff* being supervised.
- The *variety of tasks* being supervised.
- The *mix of skills and skill levels* of the staff being supervised.
- The *working environment*.

There are other variables that are not mentioned in the four cases
described in our example. These include the morale of the staff, whether
all the staff are in one location, the age range of the staff and even the
ratio of the sexes of the staff being supervised.

2.8   The Supervisor's Role – Different Views

We have already looked at the common elements of supervision and
those areas that make supervisors' jobs different. Let us now take a look
at how different levels in organisations look at supervisors and their
roles.

The manager's view

Bosses fall into two main categories: (1) those who have been trained in
management, or have acquired management skills and knowledge, and
(2) those who have been made managers for the usual reasons – technical
competence, nepotism, length of service or post vacancy – who see
'management' as a dirty word that interferes with getting the job done.

The category (2) boss, when asked what skill, qualities and attitudes he thinks his supervisors should have, rattles off a list that would make Superman, Mary Poppins and St Francis of Assisi rolled into one suffer an acute inferiority complex.

The category (1) boss has a clearer picture of what he wants from his supervisors. Here are some typical expectations:

- 'Supervisors should set a good example to their staff, keep their sections running smoothly, make decisions and keep management informed of any snags.'
- 'I expect my supervisors to sort out day-to-day problems and not let things get out of hand.'
- 'Supervisors must be firm with their subordinates, loyal to management and responsible, and keep to their budgets.'
- 'Targets must be met. That's what supervisors are for. My supervisors have to know what is going on; after all, they are closer to the workers than I am.'
- 'Supervisors? They do as they are told – they are there to improve productivity and get the best out of their staff.'
- 'Keeping costs down is the main thing I look for in supervisors. They also need to know about safety and of course all the technical details of their work.'
- 'We rely on our supervisors for training and maintaining quality.'

The subordinate's view
Now for another point of view. The following list of qualities was obtained from forty apprentices aged around eighteen years. They were asked what qualities a good supervisor should have. This is a summary of what they recorded. The quality most often recorded is at the top of the list, which then descends to qualities mentioned by at least two apprentices. (Qualities getting only one mention have been omitted.)

Supervisors should:

- Be helpful.
- Know the job.
- Be fair (also have no favourites).
- Be honest.
- Know how to get out of tight spots.
- Understand/listen to our problems.
- Be decisive.
- Talk to us so that we can understand what they want.
- Have a sense of humour and personality.
- Keep cool under pressure.

- Have authority.
- Be strict.
- Have a smart appearance.

The supervisor's view

You have read the high expectations managers have of you and the qualities that your subordinates think you should have. How do these expectations compare with those obtained from practising supervisors? Will they show a different side of supervision?

Here are a collection of answers obtained over the years from classes of supervisors in response to the question, 'What qualities do you expect other supervisors in your organisation to have?'

Other supervisors in my organisation should:

- Be able to communicate well.
- Be able to organise their staff.
- Have leadership skills.
- Take responsibility.
- Be able to delegate, control, motivate.
- Be reliable.
- Be able to transfer their skills.
- Be patient, set a good example, be fair and listen to their staff.
- Be good with people.
- Have common sense and understanding.
- Set standards for work, time-keeping, etc.
- Have a sense of humour.

There are differences between this list, the one drawn up from the manager's expectations and that of the subordinates.

Activity

1 What does your firm expect of its supervisors? Make a list from the qualities we have mentioned – and any others you think are relevant.
2 Check this list with the one you made when you attempted Exercise 2.2. How do the two lists compare? (Fifteen minutes.)

If the two lists tie up – great! If you find that you have qualities that are not being used, what do you do about it? If you find that you are short of some qualities that your job requires, what are you going to do about getting them?

The different views of the supervisor's role compared
A comparison of these three lists reveals that only *communication* is common to all three.

The managers were *results*-oriented, with all their needs pointing towards a smooth achievement of targets, goals and company objectives.

The subordinates do not have the same needs. Their emphasis is on the *context of the job*, the environment, the factors that make life comfortable for them.

The supervisors come bang in the middle of these two groups. High on their list of priorities are the *management skills* so necessary to get the job done. Lower on their list come the personal attributes that cater for the smooth running of their own sections, the atmosphere in which they work, and the relationship with peers and staff.

The boss wants the job done on time, to the right quality level with minimum fuss, economically produced, safely and with no legal or industrial relations complications.

The supervisors want the support of their peers, who should be skilled in managerial matters, and possess those personal attributes that make for the smooth progress of their own jobs.

The subordinates want helpful, honest, fair, experienced, cool, humorous people they look up to who will make their working life easier.

Put these three lists of wants together. If you can fulfil them you have the perfect supervisor. This specification would be extremely hard, if not impossible, to fill. The overall theme of all three lists is the need to move towards getting the job done *through people*.

2.9 The Tasks of a Supervisor

You will by now be aware that you are the 'meat in the sandwich' – under pressure from both above and below and often from those on the same level as yourself! Supervisors have various titles, play different roles, in a vast range of environments, amongst people who have a variety of expectations from you. However, there are common tasks to all your jobs. These are the tasks that make your work managerial as opposed to operational.

Self-check

List as many of these managerial tasks as you can. (Five minutes.)

Ideally you should have reproduced the list we drew up earlier in this chapter under 'Supervisory tasks', as these are the essence of supervision.

- Planning.
- Organising.
- Motivating.
- Controlling.
- Communicating.
- Problem solving.
- Decision making.
- Updating.

You may have listed some of them or you may have included some of your own choices not listed by us.

Because these are the jobs all supervisors must do to get things done through their staff we are going next to examine the way they *relate to each other*.

Planning, organising and control

There is a *logical sequence* that links planning, organising and controlling. No matter how simple or complicated the job, this sequence still applies.

First you *plan*, then you *organise* your resources to suit your plan to make sure that the plan can work, and finally you *control* the operation to make sure that you are achieving the targets set in the plan. The simple diagram in Figure 2.6 helps make this clear.

Fig 2.6   *The life cycle of a single job*

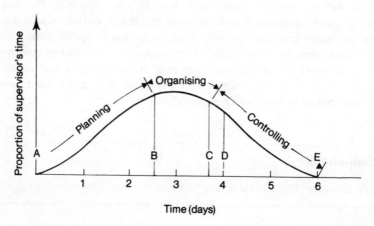

The sequence for a single job due to start at 'D' and end at 'E'. *Planning* starts at 'A' four days before the job is due to start and occupies an increasing proportion of the supervisor's time.

Once the plan is 'acceptable', *organising* begins at 'B' and carries on till 'C'.

Controlling can start at 'C' because the supervisor knows what is required and that some or all the resources have been organised. (Note that this supervisor has started controlling the operation *before it has begun.*) This control activity occupies less and less of the supervisor's time as the job progresses and ends with the job at 'E'.

Most of us have more than one job on the go at a time and more than one person to plan for. Often the different jobs and people that we are responsible for require varying amounts of planning, organising and control. The time we have to plan and organise a job is often *outside our control* – this is often decided by when our boss gives us the job, when it is required, or can be affected by problems or delays in other departments.

Motivation
The best plan in the world with immaculate organisation and foolproof controls can still cause the supervisor problems if the staff are not motivated to give their best, to get involved, to feel part of a team. How well you motivate your staff will depend to a large extent on the supervisory tasks we are about to examine.

Communication
Plans, organisation and controls are of any use only if they are properly communicated to the staff so that they know what is going on, what they are doing and why they are doing it, and only if they are told in an acceptable way.

Problem solving and decision making
Supervisors come across problems in planning, organising and controlling. Solutions are required and decisions have to be taken. How much you involve your staff in these processes will depend on your style of supervision and will also effect the motivation of your work team.

Updating
As a supervisor you have to be familiar with safety regulations and procedures. The way you carry out this side of your job will relate to motivation, planning and controlling effectively.

Christine and Gary

Some organisations work at a steady pace with little sense of urgency; others plunge from crisis to crisis where every job is completed in a state of near hysteria and panic only to be replaced by yet another job which is even more urgent!

- Christine is a senior technician and works for an international pharmaceutical corporation; she supervises four assistants, each carrying out an average of three trials in a superb laboratory complex. Working hours are 9.00 to 5.00 fives days a week. She is currently responsible for a series of tests that will continue for two years. When this is completed she will pick up another project. Occassionally she conducts short trials (one to seven days) when capacity allows. The end product from Christine's work will be on the market in five years perhaps!

- Gary works for a hospital as a maintenance engineer in charge of ten skilled operatives who cover eight different trades. They all work masses of overtime and often seven days a week. He has at any one time a minimum of ten jobs requiring urgent attention. Some jobs could take ten minutes to fix; others could take days. One job could require just one trade; another might need up to three different trades. While all are urgent, some are critical (failure could affect life and limb), others major (failure could be serious but not desperate), the rest minor. Often Gary is too hard pressed to complete a job to the required standard and has to be satisfied with getting it going. Economic pressures prevent the replacement of old equipment, and also restrict the hiring of adequate numbers of staff. Gary is an expert at 'fire fighting'. He also has a large backlog of routine jobs that have been waiting for years!

Exercise 2.3

What are the essential differences between Christine's and Gary's job?

2.10 Checklist of Supervisory Tasks

To help you help yourself we have drawn up a checklist of supervisory tasks under the main headings of people; planning; communication; control and organising.

Activity

1 Read through the list of supervisory tasks in Figure 2.7 and tick the box headed 'Tasks I do' (first column) for each task *that you do.*
2 Go through the list again and tick the box that accurately describes the *frequency* with which you perform the tasks ticked.

3 Examine the tasks you have ticked. How well do you perform these tasks? Can you identify areas of strength and weakness? (Fifteen minutes.)

Once you have done this you can decide on which tasks have *priority* for you. In general those tasks that you perform daily need close scrutiny. If you do them well – great. If you think you should do them better, these may be the ones to concentrate on.

It could be that some tasks undertaken occasionally cause you so much trouble that they require immediate improvement. Remember only 20 per cent of all jobs you do cause you 80 per cent of the problems you have. Concentrate on these vital 20 per cent and ignore the trivial 80 per cent for the time being. Once you have the vital areas under control, you can re-evaluate the situation.

Activity

From the list of tasks in Figure 2.7, extract the ten tasks that have the highest priority for you. (Ten minutes.)

Tasks I do	Description of task	Frequency		
		Daily	Weekly	Rarely
	People Dealing with my staff's problems Dealing with other departmental staff Motivating my staff Helping my staff to see the organisation's goals Dealing with customers Identifying training needs Training staff			

	Planning
	Planning work to give targets
	Planning resources – machines
	    equipment, manpower
	Planning maintenance, repair, etc.,
	    decoration, service
	Planning changes in production
	Planning budgets, costing jobs
	Attending departmental and planning
	    meetings			

	Communication Telling staff what is planned			

Calling meetings
Filling in forms
Writing memos
Collecting information

Organising
Allocating work to machines/staff
Ordering materials
Issuing/authorising materials
Issuing/authorising tools
Evaluating performance standards

Control
Maintaining records
Deciding when overtime will be
    worked
Deciding on: standards of quality,
    standards of performance, work
    priorities
Attending progress meetings
Dealing with union representatives
Ensuring standards are maintained
Maintaining safety standards
Disciplining staff
Coordinating my section's work with
    other sections

Doing
Doing operational work
Substituting for staff on routine work
Repairing equipment
Setting/adjusting equipment

Fig 2.7   *Checklist of supervisory tasks*

2.11 **Your Training Needs**

You have now ticked the chart in Figure 2.7 and identified the key areas for your attention and development. Before you dash off delving into the index to discover where you can find out more about your chosen topic, we have another task for you.

Your job is to get *results* through a *team* which is made up of *individuals*. These individuals have needs, the *team* as distinct from the *individual* has its needs, and you must get the *task* done. These three lots of needs are often difficult to satisfy simultaneously. However, the successful supervisor must do just this.

To find out just what your training needs are we ask you to respond to the questionnaire set out on p. oo. We acknowledge that the job of the supervisor is rich in complexity, but to help in your analysis, after careful consideration of the jobs of many first level managers, we have identified *twelve* aspects for you to consider.

2.12 **Training Needs Questionnaire**

We now have the framework for the questionnaire because each of these aspects becomes a *factor* that we can test by a *question*. We thus get twelve questions which can be tested by the three criteria of IMPOR-TANCE, PERFORMANCE and NEED.

We have to accept that this is a general picture, and you may like to add comments of your own to give more personal detail. You can fill the questionnaire in from your own thoughts, or you may like to discuss it first with your manager.

Please see overleaf.

Training needs analysis
Indicate by a tick where you think you stand on each scale, where
N = Nil, L = Low, M = Medium, H = High. Please add comments if
you think it explains things better.

How Important In Your Job Is	What Is Your Present Level Of Competence In	How Far Do You Have A Training Need In

1 Knowing your priorities and using your time effectively?

N	L	M	H	N	L	M	H	N	L	M	H

2 Making maximum use of delegation and allocation of work?

N	L	M	H	N	L	M	H	N	L	M	H

3 Being able to identify and analyse problems and make effective decisions?

N	L	M	H	N	L	M	H	N	L	M	H

4 Making a case and negotiating effectively to reach agreement with managers, staff and clients?

N	L	M	H	N	L	M	H	N	L	M	H

5 Showing leadership and giving your team a sense of purpose?

N	L	M	H	N	L	M	H	N	L	M	H

6 Working effectively while you are a member of a group, maintaining constructive working relationships?

N	L	M	H	N	L	M	H	N	L	M	H

7 Communicating effectively through spoken means, giving instructions, speaking to a group, interviewing effectively?

N	L	M	H	N	L	M	H	N	L	M	H

8 Communicating effectively through written means, writing instructions, memos and reports?

N	L	M	H	N	L	M	H	N	L	M	H

9 Planning and organising the work of your section, coordinating inputs from their groups?

N	L	M	H	N	L	M	H	N	L	M	H

10 Making optimum use of the resources at your disposal and understanding the financial systems within which you operate?

N	L	M	H	N	L	M	H	N	L	M	H

11 Controlling the activities in your section, budgetary control, disciplinary control, quality control?

N	L	M	H	N	L	M	H	N	L	M	H

12 Managing change and working through situations with minimum conflict and disruption?

N	L	M	H	N	L	M	H	N	L	M	H

By examing the profile of your responses in the right hand column you get a good idea of where you think your *training should concentrate*.

2.13 Personal Analysis

From the list of supervisory tasks

- You now have a clear picture of the supervisory tasks that fill your working life.
- You have rated yourself on how often you perform these tasks and probably prioritised them for yourself.
- Are you performing manual or operational tasks that your staff should be doing, other than in an emergency? If you are, should you be doing them?
- Is there any other task that you do regularly that we have not listed? Is this a supervisory task?

Further to this analysis, you now know how well you think you perform these tasks as a result of your own rating using the Training Need Analysis form. You should also know:

- How you satisfy the needs of your *individual staff* under your control.
- How you cope with your *team* and their needs.
- More about yourself and your *supervisory style and profile* than before.

From this analysis you – and only you – can decide what to do about your performance. You can work on your weaker areas. You can concentrate on areas that take up most of your time. You could make a list of your needs on priorities set against all sorts of criteria – ease of change, the effect on staff, the effect on your boss, etc. No matter how you choose your topic area, do it to suit your *own needs*. (You could of course consult your boss, a friend or your wife, to check your own findings. But, beware, they may not have the same objective as you!)

Once you have a topic area you want/need to know more about, look it up in the contents page at the front of the book or in the subject index at the back of the book. For a broad guide to your needs, the frequency of ticks under the column headed 'Tasks I do' (p. ○○) should point you to the main chapter covering that subject.

Detailed comment or fine tuning can be obtained from how you rate yourself and the skills you think you lack from your self-evaluation using the Training Needs Analysis. This should point you to the detailed information in the subject index at the back of the book.

In a book about supervisory management we have to generalise to some extent and concentrate on the central issues that affect all supervisors. You know your own field and the technical requirements needed to be a supervisor in it. This was probably why you were appointed to your present job. In this book we are concerned with the management skills a supervisor needs. Obviously supervisors need to know a lot of details about the work in their sections, but as well as this they need considerable skill in handling people and achieving the best results. We think that this requires the following main areas of skill:

- Understanding and dealing with *people* – Chapter 3.
- Getting the work done by *organising* and *planning* – Chapter 4.
- Communications skills, the ability to make yourself under-stood – Chapters 5 and 6.
- The ability to *handle information* and to *make a case* – Chapters 6 and 7.
- The understanding of the *organisation* within which you work, both its structure and its financial system – Chapters 2 and 8.
- Some knowledge of the *legal constraints* that affect your work, particularly those relating to industrial relations – Chapter 8.

In addition, you need the ability to learn from situations and to seek to develop skills and increase your knowledge.

You can use any section of the book that you think will be useful to you. They do not have to be read in consecutive order. Use this book's contents in the manner most suited to *your own needs*.

3 People: The Invaluable Resource

Management is *getting things done through people*. The efforts and results you get from your staff will vary, often as a result of how they are treated. In this chapter we will be examining the elements that come together to make an individual, the way individuals behave in groups and the problems of dealing with groups. We will look at leadership, examine different styles of leadership and, eventually, the integration of people and the supervisory function.

You can plan and organise an activity till you are certain it will work smoothly, only to find that someone will ruin it and waste your time and effort. Why is this? Is it deliberate or accidental? Is it caused by a communication breakdown?

Activity

Examine a recent problem you had at work. Was this problem caused by 'people' or 'things' or both 'people' and 'things'? (Two minutes.)

You may have answered, 'people', 'things' or both, depending on the problem you examined. This chapter deals with people and what makes them tick. Rarely are there problems that do not involve people.

3.1 The Individual

Every one of us is a complex mixture of elements balanced to make us complete, yet unique. There is no one else exactly like you, there never was and there never will be. You may feel that you are someone unique, with attitudes, feelings, expectations, skills and knowledge which are not fully appreciated by those around you. Your staff and your bosses feel exactly the same about themselves.

Let us examine some of the elements that make up an individual.

Attitudes
An attitude is the way we react in a predetermined way, or our way of looking at something. The way we react is learned from past experience and used by us to cope with the world we have met, and useful for the world we will meet.

Attitudes can be *changed*, but this takes time. Before we try to change attitudes we should know two more facts about them: they are affected by *knowledge*, and by *feelings*. We cannot have an attitude about something unknown to us. Sometimes we can change attitudes by supplying *more information*.

The last component of attitude is feeling, the emotion involved with the attitude. Often we are unaware of why we have this feeling, although we are aware that we have it. For example, some people like little children; this attitude is shown in their tendency to react to them by smiling, attracting their attention and their knowledge that past experiences were pleasant and rewarding.

The three components of attitude, then, are: a predetermined tendency towards a course of action; knowledge; and feelings. Our attitudes are what give us our *values*.

Exercise 3.1

How would you go about changing someone's attitude? (Ten minutes.)

To effect a change in an individual's attitude is not easy and is bound to take time.

Feelings and predisposition to action will change only with the acceptance of *new information* to counter existing knowledge. *You can supply this.* Once sufficient information is available to support an acceptable point of view, you could explore the area of why the individual feels the way he does, moving him towards more acceptable feelings. The need of most individuals to belong to a group will be discussed later. This group need is usually shown in the adoption of the *group's attitude*. You should concentrate on the group leader's attitude; change him and he will bring his group with him.

To get to know about feelings and the knowledge on which they are based you will have to get close to the individual. This is not easy to do, as you will be mistrusted even if your motives are genuine. A genuine interest in people and what makes them tick is a good start. But beware – it takes time.

Perception

We often see things differently from other people, thereby creating our own reality. The world does not exist in isolation, but only as *we* see it and experience it. This process is called 'perception'. Perception is what our brain does with what it receives from our senses, or how we explain to ourselves what is going on around us.

No two people necessarily perceive the same thing, while they both experience it. Because of their past experiences they may have different attitudes towards it. We have said that attitudes are our predetermined reaction to something, caused by knowledge and by feeling. If you experience something for the first time you cannot have an attitude towards it. If you have been told about it, and told that others did not like it, this may influence you to adopt a similar view.

We have all heard people say that we only see and hear what we want to. This is usually when we do not see and hear what they want us to!

Pam and Doris

Pam is a supervisor, Doris a shop steward. They are both reading the same notice on the same noticeboard. The notice is about reducing overtime due to the approach of winter and a falling orderbook. Pam is delighted as she will see more of her grandchildren. Doris is determined that this is the thin end of the wedge and redundancies are around the corner.

The words may be the same, but we all interpret or perceive them in our own context. The accountant sees lost orders as money lost, the salesman as a seasonal fluctuation. Facts and situations, then, have *relative* rather than 'absolute' meanings; our perceptions vary according to our point of view.

Fig 3.1　*Perception: an example*

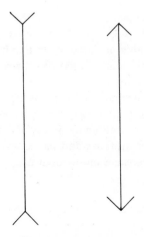

Activity

Look at the two lines in Figure 3.1. Which line looks longer?

Most people say the line on the left. They are both exactly the same length. You *perceived* the one on the right to be longer.

Activity

Here are two experiences you have all had.

1 Hearing loud pop music.
2 Seeing a large oak tree.

How did you react to them? How might others have reacted? (Five minutes.)

Your responses will depend on where you were and what you were doing at the time. **1.** You may like loud pop music – in a disco, for example. **2.** Oak trees are shady and look good on a country walk.

Other people may hear pop music as just a noise, and loud pop music as maddening, inconsiderate and vulgar. The oak tree could be perceived as a hazard to a golfer and a lightning conductor to someone in a storm.

Perception *creates reality for us*. To recognise differences in perception is to be able to put yourself in someone else's shoes – to see things from their points of view. It is important for all of us to recognise that there are other perceptions than our own.

Experiences

We differ from each other in all the things that have ever happened to us and that made us what we are. Tomorrow, because of what happened to us today, we will be different.

In experience we include all the following components: education, training, other jobs done, place of birth, upbringing, family life, religion, position in family and size of family. Every one of these components will have helped form our attitudes and perceptions and, if known, might enable people to understand more about us.

Motivation

'Drive' is that inner force, or motive, that moves us all towards a goal.

Our best efforts are always exerted towards a chosen goal. No external drive, or incentive, is ever as powerful as our own motives. A student once summed this up by saying, 'Motivation is the stirring from within while incentives are the danglings from without.'

Eminent psychologists have studied human drives and have many theories about them. The two that we will quote are Abraham Maslow and his 'hierarchy of needs' theory and Douglas McGregor's 'theory X' and 'theory Y'.

Maslow's 'hierarchy of needs'   Simply stated this theory suggests that man has a series of needs than can be depicted as looking rather like a staircase (see Figure 3.2). The most important step for you is the one you are on at any moment. The theory is that we all move up from step to step. Once we have satisfied a need, it no longer motivates us. The next step calls us on.

Starting from the bottom step, which is our lowest need, we can move upwards as follows:

- a *physiological* need, for food, water and things that we need to live;
- the *safety* need, to be kept alive and safe from harm;
- a *social* need, to belong to a group, to be wanted and loved;
- the *esteem* need, to be respected by others around us; and finally
- the *self-actualisation* need, that drives us to realise our potential, to do a good job well, and leave the world a better place.

'Theory X' and theory Y   Douglas McGregor says that people can be seen in one of two ways. The 'theory X' way of looking at them shows you a lazy, greedy cheat who must be driven hard and watched all the time. The 'theory Y' view shows man as honest, work-loving and thirsty for responsibility. Remember them this way: 'theory X' makes most people cross (X) and 'theory Y' allows people to ask why (Y), implying that this is a reasonable thing to do

Fig 3.2   *Maslow's hierarchy of needs*

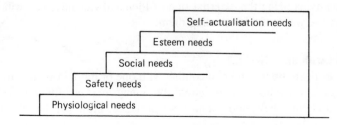

Exercise 3.2

1 List Maslow's 'hierarchy of needs'.
2 Would you prefer to work for 'theory X' or a 'theory Y' manager?
3 What are the dangers involved in using 'theory Y'?

(Two minutes for each question).

Most of us would prefer to be treated as honest, hard-working, reasonable human beings. How do you think your staff would like to be treated?

There are some people who prefer 'theory Y' treatment for themselves but insist on treating everyone else in a 'theory X' manner. This treatment usually makes the subjects behave as expected. Sometimes this is called the 'self-fulfilling prophecy'. Tell someone they are stupid and lazy and they soon will be; tell them that they can do better, and show them how, and they will.

Self-check

What are the elements that go to make up an individual? (Five minutes.)

The main elements that go to make up an individual are:

- Attitudes.
- Perception.
- Experiences.
- Motivation.

These are certainly the ones we have mentioned in the opening section about people.

'Individuality' is an idea you have probably been familiar with for some time. When dealing with anyone, if you consider their behaviour or personality as being the external sign of their individuality, you will be well on the way to understanding them.

Conflict with an individual

Supervisors are bound to be in conflict with one or more of their staff at some time or other. There could be many reasons for this conflict – discipline, behaviour or job performance. How you handle this conflict is up to you; each of us has our own methods. Below, we describe a method of dealing with conflict which is very effective.

A conflict is a clash of interest, objectives, personalities or opinions between two people, groups of people or an individual and a group. There are three possible outcomes from this situation.

The first possibility is stalemate, where both parties dig their heels in and the situation gets worse. This is a *lose–lose* situation: both the supervisor and the individual lose.

The second outcome is domination, where one of them wins and one loses. This is a *win–lose* situation.

The third outcome is compromise, in which both parties are satisfied with the outcome, convinced that they have won. This is the ideal *win–win* outcome.

Go into every conflict believing that there is a win–win outcome in it, and you will be on the way to cutting down the problems arising from conflict.

It does not matter how you bring about this outcome. It could be that one or both of you change your attitudes; it may be that concessions are made. The important principle on entering a conflict is believing that there is a *mutually satisfactory ending*. This implies a healthy, flexible attitude, and should be worked for. Not every conflict can be satisfactorily solved; there will always be instances where one of the pair in conflict is immovable, but don't let it be you. Examine your motives, experiences and perceptions.

The conflict situation is easy to see in any family home with teenagers. The differences in ages, attitudes, and status load the scene for conflict. For example:

Tom and John

Tom is seventeen and wants to wear an earring, John, his father is fifty and disapproves. John can lay down the law: 'Pierce your ear and you don't cross my door again.' He can make that stick but can he prevent Tom getting his ear pierced and leaving home? Has John won or has Tom won?
    Tom got his way, but at what cost?

Instead of this result, would John have been wiser to talk to Tom seriously and discover why he wanted his ear pierced? John could have looked around and found that there were more men with earrings than he had imagined. If John had entered the debate looking for a solution he might have accepted Tom's argument, or it is possible that Tom may have respected John's approach and decided not to bother.

3.2 Groups

Formal and informal groups

A group is a *collection of individuals*. For our purposes we will consider a formal group to be a collection of individuals deliberately formed, for a specific purpose, by the organisation for whom they work. On the other hand, an informal group may be formed by individuals from one or more formal groups for their own purpose – sport, music or a hobby which will be their common interest.

The formal group will have a leader chosen by management. The informal group will choose their own leader and, because they chose him, they will support him.

The supervisor who has a large enough section to have an informal group formed from people on his section is in a difficult situation. The people in the informal group now have two leaders: the supervisor himself and the informal, chosen leader. The supervisor will have to learn to cope with this informal leader, and often the informal leader will clash with the formal leader.

Activity

Identify a group at work that has formed, from choice, for their own purpose. (You may well belong to such a group.)

Does the group have rules and regulations? Do they keep in touch regularly? How can someone become a member of this group? (Ten minutes.)

Your answers will vary with your experience.

The group will have rules and regulations; even if they are not recorded they will be known to everyone in the group, and these will be stronger than any organisational rules. Group members will be controlled by their *desire to be a member*. Expulsion from the group will be the ultimate sanction.

Such informal groups usually meet regularly, in the pub or the canteen, where they have a special place and often special seats jealously guarded for their leaders. They may all belong to one organisational section, but more often they have a common external bond which draws them together – their hobby, interests or religion.

Entry into these groups is by invitation and recommendation only, unlike formal groups where members can be imposed. People want to join the informal group of their choice. Informal groups are sometimes called 'primary groups'.

You may have primary or informal groups on your section. Identify their leaders; get to know them and how they think. They are powerful people, as they can control their group and make your job easier.

Teams

A team is a collection of individuals with a *common goal* which is more important to them than their individual goals. If you can get your formal group working and thinking as a team you are in a strong position. To do this you need to know something more about groups and how they work.

Group dynamics

When individuals congregate in groups there is often a change in their behaviour, attitudes and goals, especially if they are united and have an informal leader. The group presents a personality, attitude and group objective of its own, far stronger than the sum of the individuals in the group. This is called *group dynamics*.

When we watch a class of male students walk down a college corridor they behave differently when they are in a group from when they are alone. The group will 'chat up' passing female students, greet other individuals or groups, and even teaching staff, in an outward, extrovert manner, unlike the individual behaviour of the group members when alone.

Group dynamics is the magic ingredient that works in a group to make them into a team. How effective this team is will depend on the behaviour within the group. We will examine some of the requirements for transforming a group into an effective team.

Self-check

How would you describe group dynamics? (Five minutes.)

You will have made the point that the *interaction* or *mixing* of individuals in the group, which makes it more powerful than the sum of its individual members, is group dynamics.

The interesting thing, for you as a supervisor, is to examine how these dynamics vary from group to group, and how they change with the task undertaken. Keep considering groups at work for yourself, and try to identify what makes them effective as teams.

3.3 Theories of People, Groups and Systems

People do not change! Theories formed fifty years ago are as valid today as on the day on which they were first expounded.

Elton Mayo

In the 1930s Mayo carried out some research at the Hawthorne Plant of General Electric which was the forerunner of all group theory. Below are listed some of his findings:

- The power of a group is much greater than the sum of the individuals' power.
- When people are given special treatment they behave differently.
- Informal groups form naturally and are more powerful than formal groups.
- The rules and expectations of informal groups are much higher than for formal groups.

Activity

Read this list carefully. Do you think these findings are still valid today? (Ten minutes.)

Do read more about the Hawthorne experiment; every serious management textbook refers to it, and it will greatly aid your understanding of group dynamics.

Systems theory

Management theories are numerous, complementary, contradictory and often confusing! The *Classical School* concerned itself with lines of authority, command and clear ideas of function and similar concepts. The *Human Relations School* followed them but were more concerned with the PEOPLE in management. Later still the SYSTEMS School came on the scene.

If you consider an organisation as a series of processes, strung together for *one* specific purpose you are well on the way to understanding Systems theory.

Taking each process as an elementary, identifiable SYSTEM, you can quite easily recognise that it has certain characteristics (see Figure 3.3):

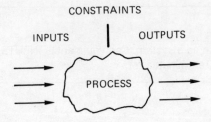

Fig 3.3 *System diagram*

- It must *do* something (be a PROCESS).
- It has INPUTS into it.
- It has OUTPUTS from it.
- It is always under CONSTRAINTS.

Often the OUTPUT from one system is the INPUT into another (see Figure 3.4).

Often several systems are *interconnected* – think of the human body with its

- Respiratory
- Circulatory
- Digestive
- Reproductive

systems, for example.

So we can say that Systems Theory is one way of representing any PROCESS by *systematically* identifying *all* INPUTS, CONSTRAINTS, and OUTPUTS that bear upon it. Its main advantage is that it often exposes details missed by less rigorous analysis.

Fig 3.4 *Output of one system as input to another*

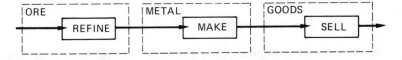

Activity

Consider your firm as a *system*. Can you identify INPUTS, CONSTRAINTS and OUTPUTS? (Ten minutes.)

Victor Vroom

Vroom used the systems approach to examine the way managers made decisions – he produced masses of useful data, theories and models.

In a nutshell Vroom's work identifies a *continuum* in styles ranging from 'solve it yourself' or 'time efficient' decision making, to 'involve the group, discuss it with them, seek their advice' or 'time investment' decision making.

3.4 Group Needs

Because groups are made up of individuals who work together to form a team for the successful completion of a task, we need to examine these three elements in the context of group needs.

- **Task**   Teams work well only when they *know* what the task is and have a good chance of achieving it. Their goal should be towards getting the task done.
- **Team**   Teams have a *need to keep together*, to be seen as a team. This satisfies a basic social need in all of us. We all like to belong to teams and preferably successful ones.
- **Individual**   The individual needs of the members of the team have to be satisfied for the individual to keep wanting to be in the team. If the individual's objectives are being continually subjugated to team objectives, the individual will become frustrated and leave, or suffer a *loss in performance*.

The way these three needs for the group are satisfied will determine just how well they perform their task. You do not, in the long term, want to achieve results at the expense of either the team or the individuals within it.

To make a team from a group we need them to work together and to achieve results, preferably the desired organisational results. This can be affected by how the group *behaves*.

3.5 Behaviour in Groups

We can examine behaviour in groups under three main headings: task helping behaviour; team helping behaviour; and negative behaviour.

Task helping behaviour
Task helping behaviour takes the form of getting and giving information, or even clarifying information and objectives which will help to get the job done. It is a healthy sign, in a group, at work or at a meeting – this is *positive behaviour*. Supervisors can encourage it and should certainly practise it whenever they are working with a group.

Team helping behaviour
This behaviour is seen when members in the group are concerned with the *welfare of others* in the group. They check that they are aware of what is going on, that they have a chance to get a word in, that they are not overwhelmed or left out. You can see this behaviour at meetings when one person says, 'How does that affect you, Carol? You haven't said much so far . . . ' This sort of behaviour moulds strong links within the team.

Negative behaviour
You can see this when a group member is concerned with *personal* needs more than those of others or of the task. This behaviour is typically displayed in cases of overtalking, repeating the same point, not listening and blocking all ideas or suggestions without offering explanations or an alternative. This behaviour frustrates the group and often results in hostility to the offender, a build-up of tension and, if not checked, an explosion of tempers. Negative behaviour is often no more than attention-seeking and may be therapeutic for the offender. Before it can be stopped you will have to find out what is causing it; the *complaint* and not the symptom needs treatment.

Activity

Examine a recent meeting where you tried to bring abut a change, or describe a new process or procedure. Can you identify all or some of the three types of behaviour we have been discussing? (Ten minutes.)

Your answer will be personal and will depend on the people at the meeting, and also on how you perceived them. They may consider the meeting in a totally different way to you.

Most meetings have a mix of all three types of behaviour from time to time. You should encourage task and team helping behaviour by acknowledging it – comments like 'That's it, you have the idea' or 'I knew you would understand' for task helping, and 'Thanks for bringing Joan in there, she's got a key role in this plan' or 'That's it, Bob, we are all in this . . . ' for team helping behaviour.

Everyone can recognise the negative comments 'Rubbish, that won't work', 'We know, we've heard it all before', etc.

Obstructive behaviour, when encountered unexpectedly, is usually symptomatic of deeper complaints. It could be that your objectives conflict, or are perceived to conflict, with the team's or individual's objectives. It could be that the resistance to change is because of fear of the unknown, in which case more information and reassurance is needed.

Another reason for negative behaviour is the 'hidden agenda' some people bring to meetings. Someone who is blocking constructive suggestions may believe that the changes being proposed could be brought in just to 'mess him about'. (See the section on meetings in Chapter 6.)

You have to be sensitive to what is going on around you, listen to what is being said, recognise and interpret the *non-verbal signals* being sent out (see Chapter 5).

3.6 Leadership

We have looked at groups, group dynamics and group behaviour. How can you get your group into a team? This is where the supervisor has to consider himself as a leader.

The word 'leader' brings to mind pictures of various leaders we have known or read about. You probably have your own ideas of what a leader should be.

Are leaders born, or can they develop? This is a question that many people ask. There are some natural leaders. The majority have worked hard, paid attention to detail, clarified their objectives and succeeded in the face of difficulty to lead extremely well.

Here is a definition of leadership: 'The ability of getting people to follow you, attempting to achieve your objectives, as if these were their own'.

Activity

List ten qualities a good leader should posses. (Two minutes.)

Everyone's ideas of a leader may be different. These are some of the answers we have had in the past. Leaders should be:

- Strong characters.
- Fair-minded.
- Respected by followers and by other leaders.
- Loyal to their followers.

- Intelligent.
- Decisive.
- Honest.
- Knowledgeable.
- Good judges of character.
- Experienced.
- Tenacious.
- Hard working.
- Able to set an example and set standards.
- Good planners and organisers.
- Controlled.
- Understanding.
- Considerate.
- Capable of seeing the 'big picture'.
- Able to communicate well at all levels.
- Charismatic.
- Self-confident.

Here are some further qualities that appear from time to time:

- Obedient.
- Hard.
- Willing to sacrifice the individual for the good of the team.
- Ruthless.

How many of these qualities did you list? How many of these did the leader of your choice have? Did he or she need them all?

You will discover that leaders have qualities that match their followers' needs. A peacetime general may be a poor wartime leader. A gangland leader will need different qualities to a church leader.

What leadership qualities do you need to supervise your staff? Have you got these? Can they be developed? How can you develop your leadership qualities? You need to answer these questions. Perhaps you will check your answers with someone you respect.

Have you ever identified the ONLY attribute every leader has? The answer turns out to be missing from our previous list – the only thing ALL leaders have is FOLLOWERS: no matter how or why, as long as you have followers you are a LEADER.

You might possess most or all of the qualities listed above and still have no followers, which means you are not a leader.

The staff you supervise, the organisation structure in which you work, and your personality and experience will all govern how you lead. These are only some of the variables.

We will look at some leadership styles now and try to evaluate them.

Leadership styles examined

Action-centred leadership   The ideal leader gets tasks done and at the same time also develops the individual and the team. This requires a *systematic approach* to your job, with pre-planning and knowledge of individual and team needs. Your objectives have to be clearly defined and compared with those of the team and individual. Consultation with your team will be vital to this style, and your skills at persuasion, listening and evaluating will all be exercised.

Not all supervisors can allow their staff to decide how the job may be tackled. Your style may be dictated rigidly by the nature of your work. Remember Mark, our operating theatre supervisor on p. ○○ – medical procedures are laid down and must be stuck to. In other jobs, processes are specified and have to be carried out.

The concept of action-centred leadership was first set out by John Adair (see his book *Effective Leadership*, Pan Books, 1988).

'Theory Y' or the consultative style   Wherever possible, you should get your staff involved in how the job should be done. People enjoy solving problems, especially when they see the benefits involved from using a solution they have helped devise.

If you *tell people what to do*, without consultation, they often react by reducing their effort or losing interest. Treat them as you would wish to be treated and they will respond to you. Listen to what they say; they often have useful detailed information that is not available to you. Encourage *feedback upwards*.

Your staff will work a lot harder on a method *they have devised* than on the method that has been in use for years. If the results achieved are the same or better, you will be rewarded by their recognition that they have good ideas and that you trust them to use them. If despite their hard work they don't achieve results, you and they have at least tried.

Give your workers feedback; tell them how you feel. Too many supervisors only complain when things go wrong. You should also pat your team on the back when they do well.

'Theory X' or task-centred leadership   We describe this style as task-centred because it concentrates on the *task* and ignores the people doing it and their needs. This style goes with the following kinds of instruction: 'Get it done, it's what we pay you for. I don't care if you don't like it, that's your problem. You don't like work anyway.' And: 'Get on with it, Julia. I'll be keeping on eye on you. I don't care how many times you have done it before; it wants doing, you were free, so you got it.'

Occasionally we all have to use this autocratic style. Except for emergencies, however, keep away from this style. It gets results fast, but what about the havoc it leaves in its wake? Frayed tempers, low morale and attitude changes which are all working against the harmony you would like to create; also, perhaps, bad workmanship.

Self-check

How best can you choose a leadership style? (Five minutes.)

You should choose a style that matches your personality, your workers and the organisation. You will, because of your attitude, lean towards a natural style. This may be towards 'theory X' or 'theory Y'. Your experience will have taught you which gets *you* results.

Your *organisation* may dictate your style; for example, would a 'theory X' style work with research chemists or 'theory Y' with hard-core criminals in a detention centre? We don't know. 'Theory Y' adherents will say treat everyone in a 'theory Y' way. They may be right.

3.7 Group and Leadership Problems

Supervisors have to keep their groups working as a team. Sometimes this ideal breaks down. Here are some problems that can crop up within the group, and their possible solutions.

Personality clashes

Individuality is expressed in *personality* – the unique way each one of us reacts to the world as a result of our perception, experiences, motivation and attitudes. Some people have stronger personalities than others. Some people are tolerant, others are not.

When you mix a group of individuals together they don't always gel. Sometimes opposites complement one another; on other occasions they bicker and behave badly.

Try to persuade the main characters in a personality clash to get on with each other. Do not take sides; instead, listen and try to get to the root of the problem and motivate those concerned to sort it out. *Use the group to help you.* Aim for tolerance, group goals, harmony, which constitute your interest in the individuals themselves.

There are four stages that stem from any personality conflict and the ensuing frustration. They are:

- *Aggression*: behaving in a 'stroppy' manner.
- *Regression*: behaving childishly.
- *Fixation*: concentrating on only one topic of complaint, being obsessed.
- *Apathy*: being uninterested.

Using these as a measure of how frustrated two people are, you can find out how serious and deep-seated your problem is. The further down the scale, the more fixed attitudes are likely to be.

If all else fails, you can appeal to the people concerned to bury the hatchet in the interest of the team and the team's effectiveness. Do not move one or other of the parties to another job early on. This could reinforce unharmonious behaviour by drawing attention to it. Reserve this as your last resort.

Performance

The *performance of a group* is a measure of their morale and cohesion. When performance drops, look for the causes as soon as possible. The change may be fatigue, boredom, loss of morale or motivation, or an external influence like change in organisation policy.

Get in among the group and tell them you have noticed and are worried by the change. Question them and find out what the cause is. Do listen to them – they may have the answer for you. Don't go elsewhere till you have done everything you, and they, can do.

The organisation and your team

Sometimes your organisation will demotivate your team by its policy or actions. This is a difficult situation. You are a representative of management and must be careful to remain loyal to them. You are also a representative of your staff.

Examine the *objectives* of the organisation that have brought about this change. If you cannot understand the reasons, find out from your peers or your manager.

Once you know the reasons for these decisions you can set about changing attitudes with additional information, expectations and all the other skills you have. Involve the team, challenge their good sense. Often, in times of uncertainty, people become insecure; they drop back to Maslow's 'safety' step (see p. oo); they worry unnecessarily. Reassure them. Do not side with your staff just to get their confidence or approval. Remain loyal to management while retaining the respect of your staff.

When you can go no further, assess the group's feelings, warn them of your intention, then go and tell your manager how your staff feel, and how you feel. They may need more resources or time; fight for them.

This may not change anything, in which case you will have to live with it. You cannot win them all.

Exercise 3.3

How can you resolve problems that arise between the members of your group? (Ten minutes.)

Brainstorming: using your group

Your staff love solving problems. The next time you have a problem, get them together and encourage them to suggest any solution that comes to mind, no matter how daft it seems.

Record all suggestions before evaluating them. Do not comment on suggestions as they are being made; reserve judgement. Often one idea sparks off another, or is built upon another, to produce a novel solution to your problem. This involves the staff, builds the team and helps you solve your problems. Don't forget to give credit where it is due.

You can use brainstorming anywhere, with any group. You can brainstorm on your own for ideas. Try it – you may be surprised at the outcome.

3.8 Supervision and People: Pulling it All Together

We have looked at individuals and what makes them unique, at groups and their needs, at individual and group behaviour and its problems. Leadership style was also discussed. The supervisor needs to know about all these topics to get the best from his team.

To conclude this chapter we would like to consider the main supervisory tasks we identify in this book (Chapters 2 and 4) and apply the details from this chapter to them.

Planning

Drawing up schedules to achieve targets. Your knowledge of the individual should encourage you to consult with your team before (or at least during) this stage, to clarify objectives. This should ensure that your *objectives* and *targets* are identical, or at least acceptable, to the team and individual needs. Keep an open mind, and if possible let the team try it their way. Remember, they like solving problems and they enjoy work, given the motivation.

Organising

Putting your plan *into action*. The workers are already involved with 'their plan'. If any of the resources go haywire they will either let you know or sort it out themselves. Later (Chapter 4) we will look at the resource side of organising.

Motivating

Getting the best from your staff. You know many ways of motivating staff. You should be able to identify where each individual is on Maslow's hierarchy (p. ○○) and able to use this to motivate him. You will have decided where on the 'X–Y' scale of McGregor (p. ○○) you should be, and be treating each member of your team in the appropriate way. The team itself will be getting your attention regarding its maintenance needs. You will be using the task itself, and the way you plan and organise, to motivate the team. They will be consulted and recognised and all feel they are doing a good job. How can you fail?

Controlling

Comparing what is *actually happening* with your plan and taking corrective action where necessary. This should become easier for you as the staff themselves helped plan and organise the job; they are involved; they will want the plan to work. Make sure that you know what is going on. Your interest is itself a motivator. When things go wrong, don't nag; put things right, make sure the mistake won't happen again and then watch over it discreetly. Trust the team; they know what they are doing (see Chapter 4).

Communicating

Telling those concerned *what is going on*, how they are doing; keeping in touch. This is another motivator. We all need to know how we are doing. You will be doing this for individuals and the team according to their needs. Tell them all news, both good and bad; tell them how you feel about things. They may tell you how they feel, and then you will have a clue to their attitudes (see Chapter 5 and 6).

Problem solving

Coping with day-to-day problems. You have help; your team will see your problems as their problems. *Use them* (refer to Chapter 1). Remember that the human side of problem solving and decision making requires you to consider the individual's needs, fears and attitudes. Each member of your team must be considered *individually*.

Updating

Keeping up to date with safety and other legislation. Share your knowledge with your team; keep them in the know. They want to know because it makes them feel appreciated when they are told of new developments. It also makes it easier to *control them* if they know the rules.

3.9 **People Have Problems**

So far in this chapter we have considered people in their work context. Often this is the only role we see them in. All your staff have private lives that are more important to them than their working life. While with you they play the role of worker, at home they are fathers, daughters, husbands, nieces, lovers. They have different roles to their work role. Away from home and work they may have even more roles to play – captain of the netball team, treasurer of the brass band, chairperson of the WI. We all play many roles, which sometimes conflict and cause us problems. These roles put stress on us, and this stress is often detectable at work.

When the staff have problems, their work may suffer, their behaviour alter, their tempers quicken. Be sensitive to your staff; notice what is going on around you. You should be interested in your staff as people quite apart from their work role. *They are people first*; work to them is a secondary consideration. Unhappy people do not make good workers. If you can help your staff in times of trouble without it appearing that you are interested only in their work performance, you will be a real leader.

People don't like mixing their private and working lives. Don't probe into their problems, but let them know that you have noticed and offer sympathy and help. They may come to you for advice, or they may go elsewhere or sort their problems out by themselves. We are all different and have different needs. Do not expect people to confide in you if you keep your relationship with your workers on a strictly business footing.

We are not advocating that you discuss every detail of your private life with all your staff. We are recommending that they do need to see you as as more than just a supervisor. Each supervisor decides how much of himself the staff are allowed to see (for counselling, see Chapter 6).

People are interesting. Each one is unique. Treat them with care. You can learn only a limited amount about people from books; your job also requires skills in dealing with people, and skill needs practice. We now suggest that you *put into practice* the knowledge that we have outlined in this chapter.

Self-check

1 Consider individuals and their make-up. What have you learnt from the book so far? Has any of this knowledge been useful to you? What can you put into practice?

- *Attitudes* – can you change them? Have you tried?
- *Perception* – does this area let you see people differently and more tolerantly? Why not check out how others perceive specific situations?
- *Motivation* – have you found out the drives of your work group? Do you know what drives you? Whereabouts are you on McGregor's scale X and Y? Can you move nearer to Y?

The above three topics should be the main factors in your understanding of individuals.

2 Groups took up the next part of this chapter. What did you get from this topic? Can you see the difference between a group and a team? Do you know what your team's needs are to perform effectively?
More than tools and resources, they need *encouragement* and *motivation* from you, together with *feedback* on how they are doing. Remember the 'task, team and individual' framework we used. You should be able to recognise the behaviour of people in groups and what it tells you about the individual. Team helpers and task helpers are to be encouraged. Negative behaviour should signal to you that all is not well.

3 Have you examined *your leadership style*? Can you change your style? Do you need to change your style?

4 *Watch other supervisors* and analyse their styles.
You should be able to handle groups better if you understand the section on problems in the group and how to handle them (p. ○○). Do you? Have you practised a brainstorming session yet? Give it a whirl.

5 At the end of the chapter we 'pulled it all together' and related all the jobs you do as a supervisor to individual and group needs and behaviour. This is expanded in Chapter 4.

Books we recommend to you:

Douglas McGregor, *The Human Side of Enterprise*, Penguin Books, 1987.
John Adair, *Training for Leadership*, Gower, 1978.

4 Getting the Job Done

The primary activity of the supervisor is to organise his section so that the work is done and the results required by senior management are achieved. This chapter sets out the stages involved in that activity. By the end of it, you will be able to distinguish between the stages and use the methods that make for more effective achievement of results.

For ease of explanation we have separated getting the job done into *planning*, *organising* and *controlling*, but in reality these three activities interact. Care is needed to remain cool under pressure and be clear which stage you are carrying out at any particular time.

As we have defined it, the supervisor's job is to get things done through people, but because that aspect is so important the people side of work organisation has been dealt with in Chapter 3.

4.1 The Process

We all organise our own efforts, and supervisors are already organising the work of others, so we should be able to help the character who first appeared in Chapter 1, Tom Stranks. Tom is in charge of a production unit in a small firm, and the other day he received a telephone call from a customer:

Tom and Part QW45

Tom picked up the phone.

'Hello, Tom, I've got a bit of a problem. Can you make 300 items Type QW45 by the end of the month to your usual price of £14.80?

Activity

List the various factors that Tom will have to consider before he can give a realistic answer. (Take your time. This requires some thought.)

This is a difficult one. You have to try to imagine yourself in Tom's position. Your list might well include these questions:

- What is involved in making QW45?
- What processes does it have to go through?

- What else have we got on at the moment?
- Can we fit this extra job in?
- Have we got the people to do it?
- Have we got the materials to do it?
- If we fit this job in, will anything else have to be put back?
- Will that cause dissatisfaction with another customer?

This looks very complicated but supervisors and managers do it every day, and quickly enough to answer the person who is at the other end of

---

Fig 4.1 *Work organisation: surroundings, elements and techniques*

Surroundings	Elements	Techniques
	Task What processes are needed? What process sequence? What methods and tools should be used?	Method study
Plant or equipment	*Time* How long will each process take?	Work measurement
	Can we fit it in with other work? (Have we got capacity?) How can we revise the schedule? Will it delay other jobs? What is the completion target?	Scheduling (Gantt charts)
People skills	*Materials*	
	Can we get the materials? Are they available from stock? Are they available from suppliers?	Stock control
Management systems	*Quality* Can we meet the required quality? How do quality demands affect the time?	Quality control
Management skills	*Cost* Can we meet the cost? Is the price consistent with the quality level and cost?	Cost analysis Break-even charting
Slow to change	*Quick to change*	*Can be learned*

the line! Tom will have to be careful not to be rushed into accepting any extra work without checking his schedules and getting the approval of his manager.

We can put the various elements in a framework as shown in Figure 4.1. In the centre box are the main questions which we all have to think through when a complex task has to be organised; on the left are listed the surrounding influences which can make the work more (or less) difficult; and on the right some of the techniques which can help the supervisor do the work more effectively.

Common elements in the organisation of work

In any case, where work has to be organised there are certain elements which *always occur.*

This framework shows the elements, but it does not really explain how the work is taken through from the initial question to completion of the task.

To see the task through the whole process we have to consider it stage by stage. To help with the explanation we have split this up into four main stages:

- *Planning.*
- *Organising.*
- *Doing.*
- *Controlling.*

These have already been discussed in Chapter 2 as the essential features of the supervisor's job.

Planning   Planning is thinking through the activities as you believe they will have to be performed to complete the task, and fitting them into a *future time frame*. To do this you need some idea of the sequence imposed by the logic of the process (you cannot put the roof on a house before the walls are erected) and the time that each activity will need.

Organising   Organising is *relating the activities required to the resources available*. This means ensuring that the people, instructions, equipment, materials and finance are available when required to complete the plan, and may involve reconciling the plan with the resources and modifying the plan until there is a reasonable fit. A crucial part of organising is communicating to all the people involved in doing the work just what is expected of them, and getting their commitment to the achievement of the plan.

Doing   Doing is the stage at which the *work is done*. Ideally this is the part of the sequence which you should not be involved in since the work will be done by the workers in the section. You should be alert to concentrating on the supervisory aspects, and not get drawn into doing the work yourself. Yet in real life the supervisor often has the expertise which is needed when the job becomes tricky, and you will have to apply 'shirt sleeve' management from time to time, and get stuck in to help the job through. You must set a good example.

Controlling   Controlling the work as it progresses means observing the work proceeds against the plan and taking *corrective action* where it can be seen that the job is not progressing according to plan. This may mean adjusting the resources (reorganising) or readjusting the plan (replanning).

Exercise 4.1

Tom Stranks's manager agreed that they should accept the order for the 300 items Type QW45. Tom got the job done and spoke to various people as it went through. Examine these statements and decide which stage they fall into.

1 'If we put the job for Bradfords back a week, we can do it.'
2 'Dave, can you start this batch of QW45s first, and I'll put Arthur on the other job.'
3 'How's the job going, by the way?'
4 'I'll set the machine up, while you get the materials.'
5 'The lorry leaves first thing in the morning, so try to get them all packed tonight, OK?' (Fifteen minutes.)

Each stage influences the others. As you know from your own experience, they often overlap considerably. To show how these overlaps affect each other we can represent the whole process of organising a job by a diagram, as in Figure 4.2.

It is important in everyday situations when you are working under pressure to keep a simple outline like that in Figure 4.2 in mind. One of the easiest traps to fall into is to rush into organising the work that you have been allocated, and to not give time to thinking through what is going to happen. If you dive into organising things without planning, you can start off in one direction only to find that you have forgotten something, or there is a conflict of two activities which you had not anticipated. Even if you are under a lot of pressure, a minute or two

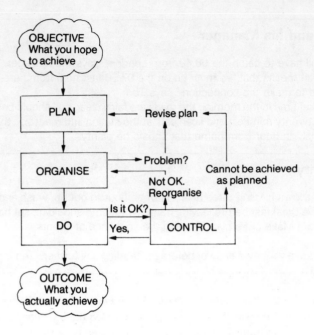

Fig 4.2 *Getting the job done: from start (objective) to finish (outcome)*

thinking through the consequences, pausing and reflecting before dashing into action, can save you a lot of trouble later on.

Having shown how planning, organising, doing and controlling relate to each other, we will now explain each one in more detail.

4.2 Planning

Planning is the stage carried out *before any action commences*. It involves collecting information about the tasks involved and getting the answers to the questions in our list of common elements.

Planning is essentially a look into the future, playing through in your mind what is going to happen or what will be required to achieve the objective under consideration, and balancing activities, resources and time to achieve the best fit.

Let us look at an example of planning. One day next week Tom Stranks and his manager are going to visit a firm to see a particular item of equipment for use in Tom's department. The firm is a considerable distance away and they have decided that it would be best to go by train. They are considering the journey:

Tom and his Manager

'We will have to catch the 08.40 from London,' says the manager.

'Which means that we must be on the 07.50 fast train from here to give us time to make the connection,' says Tom.

'At that time in the morning the roads are fairly clear, so I should be able to do it in twenty minutes, and I can park at the station and meet you there. If I allow half an hour from home that should be plenty.'

Activity

If Tom allows himself three quarters of an hour to get up, wash and shave and have breakfast before leaving home, what time should he set his alarm clock for? Make out a plan showing the sequence of events.

Write down your own answer before proceeding any further. (Ten minutes.)

We can *plan back from the key events which have to be met*. Tom must be at the local station by 07.45 at the latest to catch the 07.50 train. He has allowed half an hour for the journey and this means he must leave home at 07.15, so he must set his alarm for 06.30 to give himself three quarters of an hour to get ready.

There will be two types of plan which, although they vary in detail, will have the same characteristics:

- *List*: a list of activities with the time for each activity, drawn up in sequence.
- *Diagram*: a diagram showing the various activities drawn in sequence.

Either way, the plan is a visual representation of what we expect will happen.

List-type plan (using the example of Tom Stranks's visit)
06.30 Alarm
      Wash, shave, breakfast
07.15 Leave home
      Drive to station, meet manager
07.50 Catch train to town
      Train to town, make connection
08.40 Catch train to destination

Diagram-type plan (again based on Tom Stranks's visit)

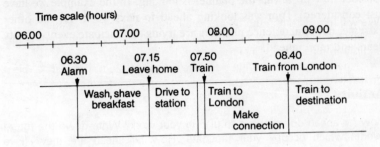

Fig 4.3 *Diagram-type plan*

Even in a simple bit of planning like this, there are some *uncertainties* and a certain amount of *estimation* has to be done. Tom's journey by car from his home to the local station will be affected by traffic conditions which may depend on the weather, roadworks or other possible hazards. Tom is making reasonable allowances by allocating half an hour for a task which he estimates will take twenty minutes. He is playing safe.

The example of Tom's trip has been followed through to show some of the aspects of planning. We would not have a written-down plan for such a simple set of activities; we would simply carry the details in our head. But as things get more complicated and more people are involved, the value of written or diagrammatic plans increases to the point where they are absolutely essential.

On a complex project the plan has two main functions. One is to *coordinate all the activities*, as we have seen, and the other is to *communicate* to the people involved just what their part is. A technique to help with more complex planning (using Gantt charts) is fully explained in Chapter 7.

As plans become more complex the facilities that computers can provide become more and more useful. Complex planning approaches like PERT (Programme Evaluation and Review Technique) are drawn up and administered by specialists, but supervisors have to be prepared to use the information produced and provide accurate data about their sections are requested.

Planning in the long term

So far, the examples we have discussed have been simple, everyday cases, but we must not think that this is the only application of planning. Planning is a process that is going on all through our work and at company level.

To put the various forms of planning into some sort of system, we can consider *how far ahead* the planner is looking. In the example we have just considered, Tom was looking ahead to next week. At the other extreme, national defence planners are trying to anticipate events twenty years and more ahead.

Activity

How far ahead do you have to plan in your work? Write down the future events which occupy your thoughts. How far ahead are they? (Five minutes.)

Answers to this question will vary considerably according to the work that you do. Most supervisors work very close to the 'do' phase of work organisation. The major planning in most organisations of any size is done by specialists, and the supervisors' job is to organise the work. They operate in the short term, thinking only days (or, at most, weeks) ahead. But there are supervisors in specialist departments where the work of the section is long term, for example in the planning department in a manufacturing company or a public authority; they have longer time horizons.

The idea of time horizons can be illustrated by imagining time stretching away into the future just as a road stretches away into the distance (see Figure 4.4). The distant future is the distant horizon;

Fig 4.4   *Time horizons*

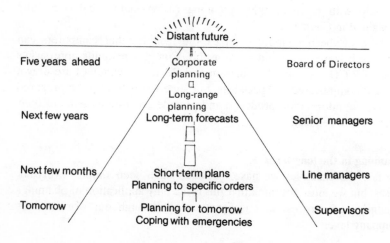

tomorrow is the road at our feet. Jobs with short horizons focus on the next few weeks, while jobs concerned with the long term tend to ignore day-to-day problems.

Most supervisors plan in the *short term*. It is the job of their managers to plan to longer time horizons. Consequently we will concentrate our attention on the short-term aspects of planning, organising and controlling.

Planning and replanning

Consider the case of a sports club or voluntary society which decides to hold a dance to raise some money for the funds. Once the committee has elected to go ahead, it will have preliminary discussions about what sort of dance should be held.

Exercise 4.2

List five questions which the committee would have to consider to outline their plans for the dance. (Five minutes.)

Information would have to be collected to answer some of these questions, and gradually the plan would start to harden up. The hall and the band would be booked for a certain date, and their charges would provide the committee with data on which to decide the price for each ticket; then the publicity could be designed and ordered. As the date of the dance approaches the details of the plan have to be filled in, such as who is going to do the catering, how the tickets are to be sold, who will be the master of ceremonies, will there be a raffle or similar competition and who will organise it, and who will set out the hall on the day.

Notice that this relatively simple project involves *many interacting factors*, and shows the true nature of planning and organising. It is unrealistic to suggest that you have a perfect plan before any action takes place. In almost every case where a plan is carried through, it is arrived at by a process of repeatedly scanning the information as more facts become available. Only after sufficient information has been collected can the outline of the plan be fixed and the final organising details be filled into this outline. Once the organisers have committed themselves to certain agreements with external agencies, then the outline has to remain fixed.

This example shows that with more complicated planning we have to recognise at the start of the planning process that we do not have all the information available. We start with a vague notion of what is required and gradually fill in the details of the plan, the times involved and the resources available. We adapt, clarify and replan as more information becomes clear and the *constraints on action* fix the key points of the plan. In this way, planning and organising overlap.

How to plan
We can write a list of points summarising how to plan, like this:

- Think through the tasks required for achieving the required outcome and work out the *logical sequence* that the processes impose.
- Estimate *how long* the tasks are likely to take and what *resources* are going to be required for the completion of the tasks.
- Fit the task sequence into *future time*, taking account of the estimated time and the availability of the required resources.
- Replan as time goes by, as *changing circumstances* impose new constraints and more information becomes available.
- *Fix the plan* as the 'doing' phase approaches, so that further changes are not allowed.

We can now look at the next stage of getting the job done, which is *organising*.

4.3 Organising

Our example of the work involved in holding a dance shows how the organising stage overlaps the planning stage. Questions raised when you come to organise things mean that you have to go back to the plan and re-examine the assumptions on which it was drawn up.

Organising is primarily concerned with deciding *how* the work will be done, what people, equipment, materials and finance are required and when they are required to be available. The other more active part of organising involves telling everybody what their part is and what is required of them, and getting their *commitment*. Organising is the primary task of the supervisor.

Exercise 4.3

Dave is a supervisor in a sports centre. In the annual cleaning programme the centre is closed for ten days so that all the facilities can be thoroughly cleaned and repainted where necessary. Part of the cleaning programme is to clean and repaint four changing rooms, each 4 metres by 5 metres, which have been emptied of all loose items. Dave has three staff under his control on one shift, and this is their task.

How should he organise the group to do the work? What factors have to be considered in making the decision? Write down your own thoughts before reading on. (Ten minutes.)

Dave will have to make a judgement, and he will have to decide whether to involve himself in the work or stay in his supervisory role.

Division of labour
Is it best to split the job up? This problem that Dave has to face represents a much deeper problem that exists in all situations where work is organised: the problem of *division of labour*. This can be seen as a tug of war between two opposing requirements. On the one hand there is the veiw that the more work is subdivided, the more workers can specialise and the faster they can achieve good results. On the other hand everyone likes to feel they are doing something worthwhile. You like to see the results of your own efforts. Consequently, if employers pursue the division of labour to extremes they create high-repetition, short cycle jobs that give the workers no sense of pride or achievement. People come to hate their work rather than obtain satisfaction from it.

The origin of these ideas lies in the work of *Frederick Winslow Taylor* who worked in engineering manufacturing in the USA in the 1890s. His approach was to study the work in a fully scientific way and he applied detailed analysis to elementary tasks such as shovelling iron ore and loading pig iron. This desire to establish 'the science of the work' lead him to break the work down into small elements. He believed that management should define the tasks in detail, set high targets, and pay high bonuses. He called his approach Scientific Management, which subsequently formed the basis of Work Study and the other management sciences. In the extreme, these principles have been used in mass production with narrowly defined, high-repetition jobs creating *alienation*. These negative effects have been critically labelled 'Taylorism'

You cannot always have a say in these matters. Methods and processes may be determined by a remote planning department or an even more remote head office, and you have to work within the instructions laid down. But you have to keep in mind that, wherever you exercise discretion over the way the work is to be done, you are designing the work that *someone else* is going to have to do. Think of the job from the operator's point of view and try to arrange the work and treat your staff so that they get a sense of purpose and achievement from their efforts. Remember the link between the task, the team and the individual outlined in Chapters 2 and 3.

Setting targets

Even if you cannot do anything about the way in which the work is divided, you can affect the way that your people view their work in other respects. You can, when allocating the work, seek to *agree targets* which the staff will take on as their own. Consult your staff to agree reasonable targets; these are more likely to be successful than imposed. Discussions like this establish a sort of contract between the two parties, and help to fix *achievable aims* for people to work towards. Having negotiated the target, the work group will be more committed to its achievement. Even in a service organisation it is possible to set targets, which, although they may be less numerical, will be targets nevertheless; for example, the speed, quality and consistency of service that customers get and the cleanliness of the service area.

All of the factors surrounding the work can be taken into account when setting targets. Think for example, of the players in a football team.

Self-check

What is the target of the players in a football team? Write down some of the possibilities. (Five minutes.)

Their target is to beat their opponents. This is a very simple and clear-cut target. It is *their* immediate target, and they will work and strive tremendously hard to achieve it. A target in the longer term may be an extension of this – to come out top of their league, which means meeting a succession of short-term targets.

If you can get just a touch of this into the organisation of the work in your section, you are on the way to improving the performance of the section as a whole.

Stages in organising

We can now summarise the process of organisation:

- Examine the tasks involved in the work, taking into account the degree of division of labour that is possible (or *desirable*).
- *Communicate* the plan to all concerned, allocating tasks to individuals.
- Marshal the necessary *resources*, ensuring that the materials and tools are available. In this aspect of organising work, the supervisor must be prepared to stick up for the staff in his section and make sure that management provide the tools to do the job.

- *Get the job started.* It may be necessary to apply 'shirt sleeve' management at this point, but avoid being drawn too much into doing the job yourself.
- *Keep things going.* Make sure that things are going according to plan (this is *controlling*) and ensure that the resources required are always available.

4.4 Controlling: 'How Are Things Going?'

Once the activity has been planned, organised and set into motion, the supervisor has another stage to perform, that of controlling what is going on. This requires seeing how things are going and *comparing progress* against the plan as organised. Then if everything is running satisfactorily, it is necessary only to continue to observe until something occurs which suggests a variation from the plan. At this point the variation is reported, and somewhere in the system action must be taken to bring events back into line with what was intended.

Self-check

Can you think of an example where control is being exercised in a way similar to that we have just described? Write down a brief outline of your example. (Ten minutes.)

There are many possibilities, including: driving a car; police control of vehicle speeds in built-up areas; stock control in a business; a teacher's control of pupils in a class.

When you are driving a car you are constantly alert to make sure that things are going as you want them to. You observe many factors relating to your progress and adjust steering, braking and acceleration to keep the car under control.

All of these and most other applications of control have certain underlying elements, which can be made clearer by looking at *control systems* in machines and mechanisms.

The five elements of control

In the building where you live there is a supply of water to the main tank in the loft. The purpose of the system is to make sure that, when you use some water in the house, the tank is refilled from the main, without overflowing. So we have a tank, with an inflow and an outflow. On its own this does not involve any true control; it requires a device to control the level in the main tank (see Figure 4.5a).

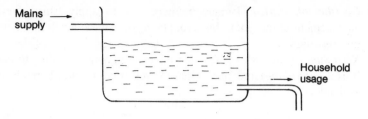

Fig 4.5a   *Inflow and outflow without control mechanism*

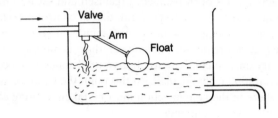

Fig 4.5b   *Inflow and outflow with control mechanism*

Fortunately we have a simple mechanism which does this work for us: the ball cock.

The ball cock consists of a float which *senses the level of the water*, and this is connected to a valve by an arm so that when the water level rises, the float rises and turns off the water supply (see Figure 4.5b).
When water is drawn off in the house, the level drops, the float drops and the supply is turned on.

This simple mechanism demonstrates the five elements present in all control systems:

- A standard (or plan) which the control seeks to keep to (*level required*).
- Measurement of the actual achievement (*actual level*).
- Comparison of the actual against the standard (*in the valve*).
- Feedback of any variances detected at the comparison (*in the valve*).
- Corrective action to bring the system under control (*valve opens or shuts*).

The ball cock is a good example of a mechanism which embodies the features that all control systems should have. We can construct a diagram which illustrates these features, and how they work together. This gives a

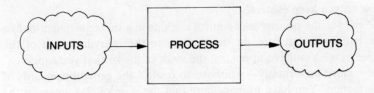

Fig 4.6   *Inflow and outflow*

general model for all control. Firstly we draw the thing that we are trying to control as a *process* with *inputs* and *outputs* (results).

If we left things like this, there would be no real control because there is no *measurement* or *feedback*. It would be rather like driving a car blindfolded with a soundproof helmet over your head! To exercise any control we need to make sure that the outputs are within *acceptable limits*. To do this, we need to measure the output, compare it with the predetermined standard that we wanted to achieve and have some way of feeding back any warning that results are not up to standard. The final stage will be to take corrective action by modifying the outputs or modifying the process in such a way that the results are once again brought back to the standard required (see Figure 4.7).

Fig 4.7   *Inflow and outflow with control and corrective action/feedback mechanism*

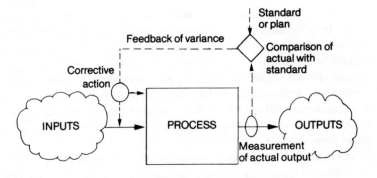

How do you keep control?
We can see the principles of control working in a simple mechanism like the ball cock, but how do these relate to the everyday work of the supervisor? You have to control the work of the section you supervise, but – more importantly – you have to control the general standards of the section. You have to make sure that the state of cleanliness of the workplace is up to standard, and that staff conform to the standards of behaviour expected in the section. In departments that serve the public this will include the appearance of staff – for example, in a retail store.

Exercise 4.4

Two supervisors in a department store were talking, and one said to the other:
    'Look at those stockings Judith is wearing. They're much to garish for a member of staff who meets our customers, and they do not conform to company rules about dress. I shall have to speak to her about it, and ask her not to wear them again.'
    List the five elements of control and match the relevant parts of this statement to each element. (Ten minutes.)

This is a difficult area for the supervisor. The aim is to maintain what you think are company standards, but to do so with a light touch, and to avoid any sense of 'I've got you under my thumb' type of control.

Limits and standards
In the case of Judith's stockings, the limits are expressed as company rules which the supervisors has had to interpret, applying some judgement. In many control applications the limits are set by management decision – as, for example, in stock control, where the maximum and minimum levels are set and routine procedures operate the control system. Similar conditions apply in other management controls such as credit controls or quality control, where the system is keeping something controlled within fixed limits. We can label this 'steady state' control since the system is working to keep everything steady *despite disturbances from outside*.

    The organisation of work presents a slightly more complicated application of control, since this is where the 'standard' to which we are trying to keep things related is not a fixed set of limits, but a plan. The plan is the thing against which the actual output is being compared. Control is still exercised, not in relation to an unchanging set of limits, but in relation to a time-based standard of progress, the plan itself. The control system tries to make sure that the outputs are following the required levels, which change as time passes. We can label this 'tracking' control.

In your work as a supervisor you have to keep the section up to standard. From talks with supervisors we can list the following guidelines:

- Standards should be communicated in as *clear a manner* as possible.
- You should *set an example*, by living up to the standards that you expect of others. Never demonstrate double standards.
- Standards (like targets) should be *reasonable*. Impossibly high standards demotivate people.
- Standards, *once relaxed*, are difficult to restore.
- Administer *corrective action* without being oppressive, using a light touch at an early warning point.
- Report *positive achievement* at least as much as failure to achieve.

4.5 Organising Your Daily Work

So far this chapter has explained how you cope with a single task, but as we know from our own experience, real life is not like that. The real life that we have to face at work resembles more a stream of activities that starts hitting you as soon as you arrive at work. Tasks do not confront you in an orderly and regular fashion; they blow up suddenly. How can you handle the daily load in the most effective way? The basic rules apply. You will cope better with things if you give some time to planning before you start the stage of organising. The plan will also give you a master to control progress against.

Given a heap of work to do, you have to start by surveying all the tasks in the heap and then deciding what the *priorities* are. This can be done only by testing each one against the statement of objectives that you are working towards. You can organise your work effectively only if you have a clear idea of *what you are trying to achieve*, or a clear statement by your employer of what is expected of you.

Activity

Write down in one or two simple sentences what is the overall objective of your present job. (This may be more difficult that it would seem. Most people take their jobs for granted. Take your time.)

How the objective is stated will obviously vary from job to job. In general the statement will take the form: 'To supervise the XYZ section to achieve the results set by management, making effective use of staff and resources, by organising the work of the section and training staff to meet the required standards'.

You can break down this overall objective into the *key areas of responsibility* which you have to take on to do the job properly. Limit yourself to six key areas and this will help you to concentrate on the most important. An example from Ian, a supervisor who looks after the final assembly shop in a manufacturing company, is laid out below to show how the two relate.

Ian's Job Definition

Overall objective
To supervise the labour in the department to produce electric motors to within a specified standards, making sure that company schedules are met.

Key areas of responsibility

1 To make sure work is carried out on time so as to achieve the agreed weekly performance.
2 To give precise instructions to the people under me.
3 To liaise with Production Control and attend the weekly forward planning meeting.
4 To give training to people in the department, when they need it.
5 To motivate, control and discipline staff in the department, as required.

It may take some time to work out a clear definition of your job responsibilities, although the task will be made a lot easier if you have a realistic and up-to-date job description. If you have one, do not assume that you can rely on it to state your objectives truly, because it may have been written for other purposes. You should be able to talk through with your manager the general outline of objectives, but not all managers are approachable on these issues. Either way, once you have a clear idea of what you are trying to achieve, you have a *reference point to test your priorities against*. When you test each task against the overall objective you can decide whether completion of the task will help towards the objective or not.

Activity

Write down five tasks that you completed yesterday. Now check each one against the overall objectives that you have previously written. Did they all contribute to the overall objective? (Ten minutes.)

This of course is another very individual test. But you will find that some of the tasks that you did yesterday may have been done more from a sense of urgency than from a sense of importance. This is shown in the case of our friend Ian, whose list of current tasks we should now consider.

Ian's Five Tasks

Ian:
- allocated work to people in the department:
- dealt with a technical problem on the assembly of a special electric motor:
- discussed with the production controller about the supply of materials for next week's work;
- helped the supervisor in the stores to identify some motors which had lost their labels;
- showed a trainee how to put together a sub-assembly on a new motor.

Exercise 4.5

Examine this list of tasks, and compare it with the Job Definition given for Ian, the assembly shop foreman. How well was his time spent? Write a short comment about each task. (Fifteen minutes.)

Inputs and outputs

When you think about the work you do, it becomes clear that work comes to your from all directions. Most likely there will be work from your boss, delegated to you as a continuing responsibility or presented as an urgent problem to be solved. Then there will be work that arises from other supervisors at your level when they say, 'Could you just help me out by getting the XY job completed?'. Finally, there will be work that comes to you from your staff, where they want technical advice, want you to get another department to cooperate on something or have a personal problem which is affecting their work.

All these are *inputs*. So how do you get it all done? The answer is that you do not do it all yourself. You delegate responsibility to the staff in your section to do the work, and some you may be able to get your boss to do. After all, if another department is not cooperating with your efforts to get the job done, it may be that the only person to sort out departmental differences is the man at the top. Your problem is to make sure that the inputs are *balanced by the outputs*, otherwise there will be a growing and never-ending amount of work which will put you under great stress. The person who works calmly, and makes sure that whatever he takes on is completed, is the person who is seen to be the effective one. The person who enthusiastically takes on new things and extra responsibilities is often the one who leaves a trail of half-finished jobs behind him. Effective supervisors are the ones who *know their priorities*, and *stick to them*.

Establishing priorities

The *job definition statement* is the master reference for establishing priorities. By relating a task to the statement you can make a judgement as to the relative priority. It is useful to use A B C categories for identifying priorities, like this.

A High priority tasks that lead to achievement of *major objectives*. There will be a real pay-off if these tasks are completed. Sometimes they may be of long–term importance but must be started promptly so that you do not eventually run into trouble.

B Middling priority tasks that are important but not so pressing as the obvious A tasks. They are the ones that can wait – but not for too long. They may be *maintenance tasks* like tidying up your work station, or *routine tasks* that keep the work going.

C Low priority tasks that could be left. For example, you may receive some selling literature that tells you of a new product. You may study it out of interest, or a desire to keep yourself informed but it can easily consume 15 minutes which would be better spent on A category work. You can check C tasks by asking yourself 'Suppose I didn't do this task – what would happen?'. If the answer is 'Nothing', then leave it.

You may not agree with our examples, the tasks in each category will vary from job to job – only you can judge what the A, B and C tasks are in your job. Your manager may have some say in the matter, and it may be useful to discuss it with him or her, but you will have to be prepared to negotiate because in some cases your A might be seen by your boss as a C. Either way, once you have a clear idea of what you are trying to achieve, you have a reference point to test your priorities against.

Effective time management comes from *editing* your work so that you concentrate on high priority activities.

Organising your day
Here are three ways to help you effectively organise your working day.

- **Make a daily 'to do' list**
  At the start of each day (or at the end of the day ready for tomorrow if that suits you better) scan through in your mind what has to be done and write down on a single sheet of paper a list of the things that you *have to do*. This can be done in any form that suits you but should be readily available at work. It might be useful to keep a separate sheet for long term projects that will take several months to complete as a 'long–term to do' list.
- **Set priorities**
  On the daily 'to do' list *identify the A, B and C tasks* and then decide which is A1, A2, and so on. If you work in a job where each task is represented by paper, as for an office supervisor or salesman, you can do this part by sorting the paper into A, B and C piles.
- **Start with A tasks not with C tasks**
  Avoid the time consuming work habit of starting with C tasks. These are often easy, comfortable, and you can do them well, but they are not contributing to the *achievement of your job objectives*. To be effective you must put your efforts into the activities which contribute to the achievement of results – these are the A tasks and this is where to start. Start a drawer for C tasks which can wait until someone shouts for them. Some will just die away and can be weeded out and binned after a suitable interval.

As you go through the day:

- **Ask the question**
  The question is 'What is the best use of my time right now?'. This was first identified by Alan Lakein in his book *How to get Control of your Time and Your Life* (1974). It is a useful question to use to check on your progress through the day. For example, when you are getting into a drifting conversation, or a badly organised meeting or you find yourself doing work that does not contribute to your overall objectives, ask the question – then do something about it.
- **Do it now!**
  Avoid procrastination. Do not put off awkward jobs till later. If you have a major A task on your list which is very important but will require large periods of time to complete and which you find difficult

to get into, this is an 'overwhelming A' and is a real problem which you may put off because you cannot find the large period of time it needs. Start it now by punching a few holes in it (this is what Lakein calls the Swiss cheese approach). *Start something*, initiate the collection of information, spend 15 minutes writing out the task stages and what you need to complete or something similar. Do it now!

Getting the job done

1 Firstly, in tackling your daily work, operate in as *calm and systematic* a way as you can. Some people like to say that they are good in a crisis, but you will often find that they ae the ones who are always in a crisis. They are not thinking ahead, not doing things systematically. It is quite possible that something you did today may have laid the foundations for a crisis which will blow up without warning in the weeks ahead. So work systematically.

2 Be clear *what the objectives are*. Be prepared to hold things for a minute and question, 'What are we trying to achieve here?' Check objectives.

3 Give *time to planning*, thinking through the possible things which might happen. Decide on the sequence of activities, what needs to be done before what, the things which might go wrong; having done that, lay out a scheme which is not overplanned. You have to leave some things to the discretion of those doing the work, and you have to leave some flexibility in the plan.

4 Take care, when organising the work, to allocate it to particular individuals, and make sure that you explain the objectives and targets as much as you can. If you can spend just a little time explaining to people what their part is and what the overall project is about, you will find that they will be more *committed* to its achievement.

5 Exercise control *with a loose rein*; tackle deviations from the standard or plan, quickly but lightly.

6 Finally, survey your own work carefully, make sure you know what *your own objectives are* in the long run. Test the daily tasks against your objectives to establish priorities. Make a daily list of things that you want to do and set priorities.

5 Getting the Message Across

In this chapter, we look at the *communication process* in some detail, in the belief that this will help you to understand how we communicate and hence become better at it!

All of us live and work with other people. In the course of this we need to know what they need from us and how they feel, while we need to let others know our needs and feelings. This we do by *communication*. We exchange ideas, hopes, information, instructions, order, requests, in a variety of ways.

Self-check

List the ways you use to communicate with others. (Ten minutes.)

How many of these did you list?

- Speaking: face to face, telephone, tapes, video.
- Writing: letters, memos, forms, posters, notices.
- Drawing: technical, sketches, diagrams, signs.
- Gestures: smiling, scowling, winking.
- Computers: use and applications.

There are some forms of communication that are not so obvious:

- The way we dress.
- The way we speak.
- The company we keep.
- Our mode of transport.

You have been communicating since you were born. Have you ever worked out how you actually got your messages across to others? Most people have not. Communication is a process which ranks very high on the list of tasks a supervisor has to perform (see supervisory tasks and personal analysis, Chapter 2).

Let us look at the process of communication as a *logical series of steps* that take you from an idea right through to getting the message across successfully.

5.1 **The Communication Process**

- **Step 1** The objective: What do I *want to happen*?
- **Step 2** The sender: How does the sender of a message *influence the message*?
- **Step 3** The receiver: Is there anything I need to know about the person who *receives* my message?
- **Step 4** Barriers: Is there anything that could *prevent* my message getting through?
- **Step 5** The medium: How should I *pass* this message? Chat, memo, telephone, letter?
- **Step 6** The tone style: Should I be *formal*? *Casual*?
- **Step 7** The message: What do I *put in*, *leave out*?
- **Step 8** Control: Does the message say what I want it to? Will it get the desired result?
- **Step 9** Transmit: *Send* the message.
- **Step 10** Feedback: Has my message been (1) *received*, (2) *understood* (3) *accepted*?
- **Step 11** Modification: How easily can I *modify* the message?

This may seem complex and long-winded to you, but, if the communication is important enough, it is worth the trouble it takes to *get your messsage across*.

Consider these steps carefully, for yourself as we discuss them in more detail.

The process examined

The objective   Are you clear about *what you want to happen*? Or are you merely concerned with *what you want to say*? There is a difference! If you are not absolutely clear about what *you* want to happen, then how can you expect anyone else to know your intentions?

Here are two examples of objectives: (1) 'When he reads this memo I want him to give me the figures I need for my production report.' As opposed to: (2) 'When he reads this memo he will know my problems.'

Self-check

Can you see the difference between these two objectives? Which one should produce a better memo? Which should get the desired result? (Two minutes.)

The answer to these questions will depend on what your *objective* was. If you need the figures for your report, then obviously objective (1) would stand more chance of getting them than objective (2), which just might get you your figures. *Be positive*.

Typical objectives

- 'I am supplying information.'
- 'I want to influence an argument with this information that no one else knows.'
- 'I want to change the way Bob feels.'
- 'I want Bob to know that I know more about this topic than Fred.'
- 'I want everyone at the meeting to realise that Bob does not know as much as he makes out.'
- 'I want the boss to know that I am the expert/specialist on computer programming.'

Many people use communication as a shield that they can hide behind. How many times have you heard someone say, 'Well, I told him. I can't help it if he's done nothing,' or 'I wrote to Jim on the 17th, what more can I do', as if this absolved them of any further responsibility? The real question should be, 'What did you do when that didn't work?'

Be clear, in your mind, what you want to happen when you communication is received. In addition to transmitting a clear message, you should be aiming at creating an maintaining a good *working relationship* with the *receiver*.

Activity

Consider any recent message you delivered or generated. What was your objective? Was your objective clear to you and to the receiver? Were there any *constraints* – of time, money, quality or authority? (Five minutes.)

The sender   The sender is a vital element in any form of communication. The sender may be generating a message or transmitting one which originated elsewhere. When we examine why messages do not get across, one factor is that the received message is often *not the same* as the one the originator had in mind! Whose fault was that? Could it be yours if you were the sender?

Examine your motives and attitudes towards a message before you send it. Are you committed to it or are you just passing it on? If you are just passing on messages like a parrot, what results can you expect?

Do you understand the *original objective*? (This makes you the receiver in a previous process of communication: should the original sender have done what we are doing now?) The sender should consider how their rank or status might affect the communication, as well as their age, experience and standing.

The receiver   The receiver of any message or communication must be clearly identified, and must be seen as a *target*.

You have to give some thought to this element of communication if you really mean to become effective. What do you need to know about the receiver? You must first of all decide whether your communication is for one specific person, for several or for a large number; know their age, intelligence, experience and position in the organisation. For example, would you treat someone of your own age, and at the same level in the firm, as you would an unknown outsider?

Communications are often addressed to many people when they are in fact only meant for one specific 'target'. These communications lose their impact and often cause more hassle than they are worth. Take the example of lateness by one or two employees being dealt with by a memo to all staff about time keeping. Does this stop the culprits, or alienate the innocent?

Another area to consider with regard to the receiver of the message is that of *background information*. Does the receiver know the context of the message? Or is it isolated and unrelated to other factors that would make it more acceptable? Should you zip it up for him by telling him the other relevant details?

Exercise 5.1

List ten details you should consider about the receiver of your message,. (Five minutes.)

Barriers   There are always numberous barriers between the sender and the receiver(s) of any form of communication. These barriers are anything that may prevent the message 'getting across'. We sense these barriers, but perhaps we have never got down to listing or examining them in any detail. Let's do that now.

A simple way of thinking of these barriers is to put them under two broad headings, 'internal' and 'external' barriers. Let's say that internal barriers are those *inside the communicators* themselves and that external barriers are *outside them in their surroundings*.

1 Internal barriers   These include feelings, attitudes and perceptions, which all go to make up the *intrinsic personality* of the individual. All of these can influence communications. Perception is a typical example: if the sender perceives a piece of information in a certain way, and does not appreciate there may be other viewpoints, a barrier is created. This applies equally to the receiver(s), who may themselves 'see' the message in different lights because of their perceptions. This can cause confusion and act as a barrier.

There are *physical barriers* to communication: cleft palates, deafness, poor sight, illiteracy or educational deficiencies, that hinder the smooth flow of communication.

People have their own idea of their role in life, their position in the scheme of things. Often their ideas do not conform to the role or position that others *see them in*. This can also prevent the message getting across.

Basic intelligence governs our ability to grasp new ideas, hence this *level of intelligence* must play a part in communication. Unclear speech, a heavy accent, the use of slang or jargon can all get in the way.

2 External barriers   Have you ever tried passing a message to someone at a noisy party, dance or disco? The *environment* is often a barrier. Distractions can create barriers through the eyes, ears and mind. Incidentally, in some cases, the actual method of communication distracts the receiver from the subject – fancy script or letter paper, an accent even, may detract from the message.

The *organisation structure* can itself create barriers because of the levels within it. Physical distance is a barrier; dislike of the medium of communication selected is another. If there is an 'atmosphere' caused by something outside your control, this may get in the way of communication for anyone subjected to this atmosphere.

The *language* used in any communication can be a barrier, or a lubricant to smooth things to their desired conclusion. Consider the effect of technical jargon, or even complex grammatical constructions, on the flow of information. Often the sender might just as well talk in Swahili for all the good it does. Keep it simple.

The medium   There is always a choice open to us as to *how to communicate*. We can speak, write or combine both if necessary. It's up to us to choose the medium that best suits our objective. Sure, there will always be constraints: time, availability, cost. This does not absolve us of the need at least to consider and evaluate the possibilities available.

Should we write, or phone? Would it be better to pop round and have a chat to explain what is needed? Often a few moments invested at this stage can prevent calamities occurring later on.

The *medium* is often as important as the message. Complex information needs to be written, if only for the purpose of record. On the other hand, why write when a few words on the telephone, over a cup of coffee or in the corridor may be more appropriate? Remember, some things we say take on a totally different dimension when written.

Have you noticed that some people cannot describe anything without waving their arms around, others draw sketches to help their explanations, while there are those who copy down everything you say? Remember that people around you may favour a different medium from the one you normally use.

Activity

If you were directing someone to a location a mile away, how would you go about it? Would you:

- Draw a map?
- Describe the route orally?
- Write down directions.
- Perhaps combine two or more of the above methods?
- Check the traveller's knowledge of the area?
- Make sure they understood?

(Two minutes.)

Remember, not everyone can understand sketches, plans and diagrams. Similarly, long descriptions can confuse others. You can try various methods to suit the *needs of the message and the receiver*. This will improve your communication skill.

The way we *present* information dictates how easily it is understood and accepted. A little thought will help you to select the best medium for the task in hand. We recently tried to convince a colleague that changing offices would be to our advantage. Long descriptions of the new layout failed to make any impression. A scaled drawing on graph paper quickly convinced him that he would have more room and that storage space would be much more accessible.

Should you present production figures in tabular form or would they be better shown in the form of a graph? In the section on techniques (Chapter 7) we demonstrate various methods of presenting information.

Tone and style   Once you have considered your objectives, the people involved, the barriers that may exist between them and, eventually, the medium you wish to use, you come to yet another important area forconsideration: the *tone or style to be employed*. This aspect of communication must be selected to fit the objective and the person concerned, as well as the medium selected. All these must be integrated to give a harmonious balance.

Does the communication need a formal approach? Is there a standard form or procedure you can use, or should you be informal? Once this has been decided, move on to the tone you want to project. This is an area often left until too late, because of lack of thought.

How many times have you written a letter and, on reading it through, felt uneasy about the tone? The words seem to be all there, but somehow the tone isn't quite right. What a waste of time!

Exercise 5.2

How many ways could you get the following message across? 'Sweep that floor now.' (Ten minutes.)

Can you see what we mean? The tones and styles vary; only you can decide which would be appropriate.

Read the following passage through:

'The small domesticated carnivorous quadruped member of the genus *felinus* was in a position in which its body was supported in a more or less upright position which its buttocks resting upon an article manufactured from fibrous extractions of coir and plaited rush-like materials.'

This could be said in six words: THE CAT SAT ON THE MAT

Of course no one in their right mind would use the long-winded, rambling paragraph above when they could make the point in one clear, concise sentence. Are you sure of that? Unfortunately we are all of us often guilty of padding and complicating our messages, for one reason or another, and to varying degrees.

- Keep it *simple* and to the *point*.
- Make sure the *style matches the need* and think about the *tone* you are using.

Remember why you are communicating: *you want something done.*

Activity

1 Identify the different styles your bosses, other supervisors and your family use.
2 Evaluate these styles and their effectiveness. (Ten minutes.)

This is quite a task to undertake. If you persevere with it, you will learn a lot about this important element of communication for yourself.

The message This is the focus of all communication – the bit that actually survives. It can be *heard*, *seen*, *read*, *referred to*. All the work we have done till now may not be appreciated, but it will certainly alter the effectiveness of your communication. Often, we go through steps 1 to 6 in the process without realising that we are doing so.

For any message that we transmit, we have a choice as to what it *contains* (too much information can be just as confusing as too little). The secret of effective communication is to put in just enough information to get the message across to the receiver selected, without overwhelming him with irrelevant data. On the other hand, we must be sure that we don't miss out anything that is needed.

Check that the message is clear, easy to understand, addressed to the receiver and contains all the constraints that apply to it. This means that the receiver knows clearly what action is expected, when, where, by whom, at what cost, etc.

Control We stated that the process of communication started with having an objective. This objective detailed what you *intended to happen* as a result of your communication.

Once you have 'the message', you should examine it carefully to see if it will in fact achieve the result outlined in the objective. If you are sure that the objective can be achieved, all well and good. However, should there be any doubts, this is the time to consider why the objective may not be achieved.

Failure to meet the objective could be due to a weakness in any of the steps we have already examined. Look again at *all* of them to find out where the fault lies. Could it be that you had misjudged the receiver? Could it be the barriers? Could it be the medium? Could it be the tone? Could it be the message? Once you have spotted the weakness, you can put it right.

Now compare your message with your objective, and if it's likely to achieve it, you can proceed. If not, keep at it until it does! There's no point sending (transmitting) any communication that you do not think will work, so you may as well work at it until you, at least, believe that it will.

There's never any guarantee that we can get the message across. All we can do is go through a process that should get the message across; this we owe to ourselves and to those with whom we communicate.

Transmit   So now you have a message that you think will meet your objective. You have considered the receiver, the tone, the style and the medium you have selected. Go to it – tell them. Whatever the medium selected, be clear, concise and genuine. Tell them and await results.

Feedback

1 Evaluating feedback   The message has been transmitted. Now what? We are awaiting results. To speed things up we should *evaluate* feedback to see how the message is being received. Remember our objective: we wanted something to happen.

Once our message has been transmitted we need to know that it has been received. This is the least we need to know. What point is there in transmitting messages which never arrive?

Once we know that the message has been received, what next? Surely, we don't just want to know that our words were heard or read. We want more, we want to know whether our words have been *understood*. If we are not understood then what point is there to it all? Surely we must ensure that our message is accepted. How can it be carried out if it is not understood. How can we ensure it has been accepted? Why not build a *feedback loop* into our communication? This allows us to check that the message has been received and understood.

Why stop here? Why not progress to the ultimate in feedback: has the communication been actioned? After all, this is what we set out to achieve. Build feedback into your communication, check receipt, understanding and action.

2 Feedback methods   How can this be done? Let us examine how we deal with a young child about to go on an errand to the corner shop. The child is being sent to buy a 2 lb bag of sugar. Let us concentrate on the specific area of feedback.

The child is about to depart clutching the money in its sticky little hand, together with a written note (just in case things go wrong!).

Activity

How can you make sure the child will return with 2 lb of sugar? (Five minutes.)

These are the questions you would ask: 'Now, what are you going to buy? How much will it cost? How much change will you get? What will you do if you forget what to say?', etc. Only once we get the expected responses will we send the child on its way! This process will tell us that the child has heard, understood and is about to act on our communication to our expectation.

Would there be any point in asking, 'Do you understand?' People – including children – don't like to say they don't understand, and often say 'yes' when in fact they do not understand. What we need to know is that the child does understand and can demonstrate this fact by describing the actions that are required.

3 Build feedback into your communication Watch for signs when communicating orally, face to face. Frowns, fidgeting and wandering eyes all tell a story to the vigilant. The answers to questions such as, 'How will results be achieved?' 'What methods will be used?' 'When is completion expected?' all tell you much more than 'Do you understand?' or similar questions.

Modification Make provision for modification to your communication should it be necessary. If a provision for modification is built in or even considered, it will be *easier to implement* than if a modification is just tacked on as and when necessary.

This modification may be an alternative message, addressed to an alternative receiver, the use of another medium or maybe in a different style. It could be one or a combination of these changes, still with the same objective in mind.

Exercise 5.3

Consider how you communicate, and try to identify which steps you take and which you omit. What can you do to improve your communication process? (Ten minutes.)

The process discussed above is an ideal model, and as such would apply to any type of communication. Concentrate on those areas of communication where everything has to be exact to guarantee the message getting across, where failure to do so would be catastrophic.

Activity

The next time you see a product advertised, examine the advertisement critically against the model process we have used. Consider it step by step and you should see what trouble has been taken to 'get the message across'.

The advertising industry spends thousands of millions of pounds on their advertisements, employing highly skilled specialists to do just this. Effective communication is never easy, but always worth the effort in saved time, improved understanding, higher morale and numerous other intangibles.

This process should form the basis of communication at meetings, interviews, when you are giving a talk or producing a poster – any time or place we wish to communicate. The steps will assume varying priorities for each use, but they will all have to be used to get you to a position where you can *get your message across*.

Activity

Select any example of your written communication and initially examine it using the process above, going through it step by step
1 Could it be improved?
2 Pretend you never sent it – compare the message with your objective – rate your chance of achieving it.
3 Rewrite the message, using the steps we have just discussed.
4 Now rate your chance of achieving your objective.

(Ten minutes.)

5.2 Types and Uses of Communication

We have already agreed that supervisors differ in their tasks and responsibilities, but they also have certain common tasks which they all perform. By the very nature of supervisory work, they all *communicate*. Just how much they communicate varies with their role. Research shows that the average supervisor spends from 50 to 80 per cent of his working day communicating.

Activity

Check how long you spend communicating in your job – you may be in for a surprise. (Ten minutes.)

This is a typical breakdown of the time spent on communication.

Type of communication	% of communication time	% of working day
Listening	45	36
Speaking	30	24
Reading	15	12
Writing	10	8
	100	80

The exact amount of time we spend on each of the activities listed above will vary from day to day and from supervisor to supervisor. These changes should not change the ranking of the four types of communication, except for some extraordinary jobs.

Activity

We have ranked four types of communication in order of time used. Consider your communication at work and give priorities to these four activities according to their value in your job. Your list should tell you something about how you communicate at work. (Ten minutes.)

It may be that although *writing* occupied the least of your communicating time it was the most vital aspect of your particular job. For some of you *reading* could be the vital aspect that you need to concentrate on. Only you can make this judgement. In the following pages of this chapter we will examine each type of communication in turn in general terms. In Chapter 6 we will examine the specific applications of these four broad categories of communication.

Listening and *speaking* are the two complementary halves which together make up *oral communication*. Between them they take up 60 per cent of our working day. If we can make even a small improvement in our oral communication, then this, spread over such a large chunk of our life, will soon pay dividends in improved performance.

Just as listening and speaking combine naturally to form oral communication, reading and writing combine under the heading of *written communication* and may occupy 20 per cent of our working day.

5.3 **Oral Communication**

Listening

Let us consider this first as we spend so much of our time listening. Most of us are not very good listeners. This is mainly because we have never been taught to listen.

Hearing is not the same as *listening*. Listening is what we do with what we hear. Listening is difficult and requires active participation on your part. Watch someone who is really listening to a favourite piece of music; compare this with someone watching television and 'listening' to a conversation simultaneously. Could you spot the difference? The real listener had to make a conscious effort to listen and not just to hear.

Listening is to hearing what perception is to seeing (see perception, Chapter 3). Our listening efficiency is often very low, and this problem is compounded by the fact that we could be spending more than one third of our working day listening. Any improvement in listening must make us better communicators.

Self-check

Why are we bad listeners? (Think about this before writing your answer.)

Here are some reasons why we are bad listeners:

- Listening involves *effort,* and we are lazy!
- Listening is *difficult*, and we tend to underestimate this fact.
- We think *we know what people are going to say.*
- Our *concentration wanders*.
- We are *easily distracted*.
- We hear *what we want to hear*.
- We are used to 'easy listening' on television and radio, and *do not make the effort* with ordinary folk when the going gets tough.

Remember that you are responsible for what you do with what you hear – it is no good blaming the speaker. You can improve your listening by overcoming the bad habits you have probably accumulated as the result of not being taught to listen.

How to improve your listening   Let us look at some of these stumbling blocks and their cures.

- Often we are thirsty for facts and are so busy grasping at these that we miss the *idea behind the fact*, thereby missing the main argument or theme. Once we get the drift of an idea and really grasp it, we can quickly fill in the details. The chance of fitting ideas and themes to facts is not quite as easy. So go for the idea and really understand this; the detail will fall into place. Example: ask anyone the date of the Battle of Hastings, '1066' they will all reply. Then ask why this date was important? Are the answers as clear?
- Do not confuse the speaker with the subject under discussion. Tom may be an old bore, but he may have a very valid point to make. You may miss it if you confuse him with the subject he is talking about. Hear him out. Judge his content, not his delivery or prejudices.
- People get emotionally involved. Keep cool; do not get involved; analyse what is being said; try to understand why you want to lose your cool.
- Distractions are all around us. We *can* decide whether we allow ourself to be distracted: concentrate; filter out sounds and movements; you can if you try.
- Do not dive in too soon; hold your fire until you understand what is being said. Premature interruptions prevent you grasping the ideas being developed and often wind up the speaker.
- When the going gets hard, do not pack up and switch off; work hard to try to keep with it. You can practice by deliberately listening to people who are *not articulate*. Let them finish what they are saying, then summarise what they have said. Check that you have really listened by their reaction to your summary.

Use your thought speed to your advantage   The average human thinks fives times faster than he speaks. Because of this we are usually miles ahead of the speaker we are supposed to be listening to. Instead of using one fifth of your capacity to hear what is being said, concentrate, listen, analyse what is being said, watch for gestures, tone, facial expressions. This will occupy your slack capacity and make your understanding of what you listen to more *personal*.

Speaking
We spend something like one quarter of our working day talking. This time is shared between: giving information, collecting information, instructing others, chatting, interviewing, meetings, training. The process of communication previously discussed applies to all of these

activities. The objectives will vary and so will the importance of each step, but the process will still hold good.

Exercise 5.4

What advantages of using oral communication can you think of? (Ten minutes.)

Activity

Do you think that there are any special skills required for oral communication? (Five minutes.)

While the general communication skills apply, oral communication also requires:

- *Clear* speech.
- *Simple presentation and style*.
- *Logical flow* of ideas.
- Frequent *summaries*.
- *Concise delivery* – keep it short.
- *Eye contact* to receive feedback.
- Opportunities for *questions*.
- *Patience*.
- *Listening skills*.
- Quick reaction to *feedback*.
- The ability to *restate* the communication.

5.4 **Written Communication**

Writing

Writing needs particular attention because it may be used in evidence against you. So be warned – get it right! People may not remember exactly what you say (because they do not listen!), but they do retain the general drift of your statement. They can always *refer* to your written words.

The communication process applies just as it does for oral communication; the *objective*, *sender* and *receiver* steps remain unchanged. When considering *barriers*, be conscious of when and where your communication will be received, and the effect this may have on its reception. *Tone* and *style* are vital to written words and must match the *objective*.

Keep written work simple, clear and to the point. Do not use long involved sentences (a good rule of thumb is about twenty words to a sentence). Try to keep just one topic to a paragraph. Use commas sparingly; they can easily alter the sense of your message. Be assertive, not aggressive or servile. Be firm and positive; let people know what you feel. Commit yourself, do not hedge, state your case and your reasons for putting it.

Avoid jargon and clichés wherever possible. 'At this moment in time', 'as we know it today', 'ongoing situation', all deserve instant deletion from any message!

If you have to write longhand, try to write legibly. There is no point in writing if your script cannot be read. Remember the *receiver* and why you are writing; you will not achieve your objective if the receiver is wound up because he cannot read your scrawl.

Here are some examples of written communication which supervisors send and receive: letters, memos, notices, reports, projects, specifications, instructions.

Reading

You would not have got this far in the book unless you could read! You have done it for years. Do you take everything you read at face value? Is it all black or white – or are there shades of grey? Do you try to get into the writer's mind, to try to work out what his objectives are? If the writer is an excellent communicator then your job is made easy. What if he is not – how can you help yourself?

Check that the message is clear, then check if there is possibly another message there. If there is any ambiguity, check it out. Does the *context* of the message help to clarify it? Think of the writer (the *sender*, step 2 in the process of communication). Does this give any guidance? If you are still unsure, get in touch with the writer and clarify the message.

There are many ways we can improve our reading. Here is one. Skim through and get the drift or idea. Then go back and fix the details clearly – dates, times, prices, etc. Often if we concentrate on every word we miss the vital objective while retaining details of data, and subsequently not really understanding what is being read. Another tip to help you once you have read a written passage is to underline or block in the important passages with a highlighting marker to make them clearer and easier to find.

5.5 Non-verbal Communication

We all communicate a tremendous amount without saying or writing a single word. Our expression, gestures, posture and clothes all telegraph messages long before we speak. Be aware of this and make sure that you are 'saying' what you intend to. Often we contradict our words by our actions, which confuses people around us.

Be conscious of non-verbal communication around you. Be sensitive to tone of voice, eyebrow positions, clenched hands, eyes that do not meet yours. All these are symptoms of feelings that could be barriers blocking your message.

There is not enough space in this book to delve into the finer points of NVC. However, there are two excellent books you can read on this subject and these are listed at the end of the chapter.

Activity

1 List the NVC signals you pick up from people around you.
2 How can you tell if someone you cannot hear talking is sad, angry, tired, etc?

(Five minutes.)

1 The NVC signals you should be able to pick up are easily seen in people's faces: frowns, smiles, raised eyebrows, heads bent to one side, are typical examples. Heads hung low, clenched fists, fidgeting, rigid postures all tell a story. How good you are at 'reading' these messages will depend on your *sensitivity* and *experience*. This valuable feedback will help you communicate better.
2 You should be able to judge all these conditions from both *expression* and *posture*. Notice how people signal their feelings. Check your judgements with the subjects under observation if you can.

5.6 Electronic Communication

Earlier, we broke 'communication' down into two categories:

• speaking/hearing.
• writing/reading.

Recent years have seen the introduction of electronic production of both these forms of communication:

Oral: Have you come across synthetic speech generation? Cars that warn you that your seat-belt is undone, machines that inform you that they are empty, unavailable, etc . . . . This is different from machines that pass on human voices pre-recorded and broadcast on the activation of some form of trigger.

If you are initiating this form of communication, are there any special problems you should consider?

- Do we like this form of communication?
- What can we do to make it more 'user friendly'?

Your answers will depend on your age, culture and environment.

Written: It is commonplace these days to receive electronic messages from:

- hole-in-the-wall money machines
- stock-control systems
- automatic test equipment (ATE)
- computer generated data, such as rate demands.

How does this sort of communication affect you? Does it require special consideration or is it subject to the same rules as 'ordinary' communication?

In Chapter 6, we will be looking more closely at *Information technology*.

We have covered the process of communication in this chapter and identified the ways in which supervisors communicate. To check that you have understood what we have written we recommend that you attempt the following.

Self-check

Consider all the steps in the communication process. Identify the skills a supervisor would require, to carry out each step effectively. The skills you have identified should match those listed below.
(Ten minutes.)

5.7 The Skills of Communication

How did you get on? Let us use the process we are now familiar with to identify the skills required for effective communication.

- **Step 1 Objectives**
  This step requires *analytical skills*, the ability to *reason clearly* and the confidence to know *what we want to happen*.

- **Step 2 Sender**
  Here we need to know about *ourselves* – our strengths, perceptions, weaknesses, prejudices and personality, as all these affect our outlook on life and subsequently our communication style.

- **Step 3 Receiver**
  Our *interactive skills* are heavily in demand here. How well we know other people will govern our success with the communication process. 'Know your receiver' must be the motto for all aspiring communicators. Putting yourself in the receiver's shoes will help. Feeling as he feels, thinking as he thinks, knowing his background, experience and intelligence all help to get the message across.

- **Step 4 Barriers**
  An ability to establish a *relationship between you and the receiver* is a good start at this point. Sensitivity, understanding and consideration will all help to identify the possible barriers. Analysis, planning and evaluation should help to overcome the barriers detected.

- **Step 5 Medium**
  To handle this step involves knowing the *media available*, knowing the value of each medium and being able to match a medium to the message.

- **Step 6 Tone and style**
  The skills here are similar to those required in steps 2, 3 and 4. Other skills required are the ability to recognise differences in tone and style and then be able to generate these on demand; control over the use of emotionally charged words and phrases; the ability to select the *appropriate language*.

- **Step 7 Message**
  The ability to write, talk and act accurately to the dictates of steps 1 to 5. Having command of the *medium of language* – keeping it simple, concise, accurate and clear. Acquiring the appropriate *vocabulary* needed. The ability to distinguish the relevant from the irrelevant; to get priorities right; to present data in a logical order; and to keep the message as short as possible without losing the sense of purpose.

- **Step 8 Control**
  Here you will need to evaluate the chances of getting your message across. If you decide your chances are low, then analysis will help you to find out *why*.

- **Step 9 Transmit**
  Varies with situation, medium, receivers, etc., but must always be *clear*.

- **Step 10 Feedback**
  The skills needed at this stage are the ability to recognise and interpret NVC (for oral communications) and the ability to put questions in a

way that provides the sender with information on the *receiver's reception, acceptance and intentions*.

- **Step 11 Modification**

  This last stage calls on your ability to evaluate different messages, objectives, barriers and media, and to slot in changes *to suit the existing need*.

Now we have looked at the process of communication, we can move on to how we use the process in Chapter 6.

These are some books we think will help you understand more about non-verbal communication:

Desmond Morris, *The Naked Ape*, Panther Books, 1981.
Desmond Morris, *Man Watching*, Panther Books, 1978.

6 Applications of Communication

6.1 The System

In Chapter 5 we discussed communication as a process and identified the ways in which people communicate with one another at work. In this chapter we will show how the process of communication is put into practice. We will examine communications in the firm to outline the general picture, and later concentrate on the supervisory applications of communication.

When things go wrong you hear the cry 'another breakdown in communication'. While some problems are caused by poor communication, there are many other reasons for failure. Because supervisors spend so much of the time communicating, we feel that this area is worth concentrating on to improve supervisory performance.

Management is defined as 'getting things done through people'. Supervisors are the first line managers and they are responsible for the actual operations, or 'doing' the job. They need to communicate exactly *what* things require to be done, *by whom, where, when, how* and often, *why*.

Your organisation has a system for passing information around its various departments. This system may have been specifically designed as a communication system; more likely, it developed over a period of time to suit the needs of the departments through which it passed. Often there are several systems in operation.

Activity

Make a list of the different ways in which you receive information of work. (Ten minutes.)

You will have probably listed some, or all, at the following:

- Letters.
- Notices.
- Memos.
- Forms.
- Registers.
- Meetings.

- Returns.
- In casual conversation.
- Progress information – costs, wages, sales, scrap.
- House magazine.
- By word of mouth from someone in the know.
- Rumours.
- Gossip.
- By finding out for yourself.

When you examine your list you will probably recognise two different types of communication: the *formal* type controlled by the organisation – letters, instructions, memos – and all other communication not controlled by the organisation; and the *informal* type, called 'the grapevine', which includes information passed by word of mouth, rumour and gossip. (See Chapter 8 for formal and informal ways of getting things done.)

You have probably heard comments like these at work:

- 'Old Bill in planning always knows what is going on, let's ask him . . . '
- 'Mary in the typing pool always keep me in the know.'
- 'Tom's brother plays darts with Jim and he warns me on Fridays if there are any changes.'
- 'Everybody knows that Jean in Costing is the only one who understands this system; go and see her.'
- 'The liftman told me about it . . . '

Your examination will probably have led you to recognise that communication systems are set up for the benefit of the departments that set them up! Often you pass on the information in different ways to the different departments with which you deal.

Firms are in business to get things done, and they organise their resources to do this. Departments are organised to work efficiently, but communication systems are seldom designed into an organisation. Every organisation should pay careful attention to how the information *passes through the system*, and not assume that the routes originally laid out are being followed. Many of the day-to-day problems you encounter are caused by this casual information routing.

Self-check

What are the dangers of the informal communication system? (Five minutes.)

Often the informal system transmits information that is out of date, distorted, misleading or incomplete. Because it cannot be controlled it can cause problems to you as a supervisor; for example, serious misunderstandings can occur when you and your bosses assume that formal information channels are being used, while staff are in fact using 'the grapevine'.

6.2 Communication Systems in the Firm

When examining communication systems, three questions must be asked, and *answered*.

- *Is there* a system?
- Is the system being *used*?
- If there is a system and it is being used, is it *effective*?

Ideally every single person in the organisation should get the right information, at the right time and in the right form, if they are to do their job effectively. This does not happen by chance. It takes careful thought to identify what information each person needs to do their job, to plan when and how they will get the information and, finally, to get it to them.

Some firms believe the way to solve communication problems is to flood everyone with masses of 'bumph'; unfortunately this is just as bad, if not worse, than too little information. This 'information overkill' can have one of these two undesirable outcomes:

- People tend to ignore all communication, because most of it does not concern them.
- People spend too much time reading everything passed to them, whether it concerns them or not.

There is usually an organisation chart for most firms. This chart was probably designed for the control of the various functions within the organisation. These routes created for organisation and control are often used for communication purposes even though they may be far from ideal for this purpose. They often *hold up communication* because they are so cumbersome to use.

An alternative system
Some firms have recognised that passing information along the lines laid down on organisation charts is time-consuming and inefficient. An alternative to this method is the use of *briefing groups*. Under this system the whole organisation is carefully examined and broken down into groups of people, by rank, location or function; then the groups are

briefed, and they in turn brief other selected groups till the whole organisation has been covered. The timings, locations and attendance of these meetings are carefully planned to maximise efficiency and minimise the time taken to pass on information.

Activity

Identify what information each of your staff requires to do his job, when it is needed and in what form. (Ten minutes.)

Do the same for your peers and your boss. (Ten minutes.)

This may have been a challenging task to complete. It should be worthwhile, as you now have a clear picture of the communication needs of those around you. Do all these people get the information they need? If they *don't*, you may be able to put this right. Find out what information *they expect from you*.

If you found this activity difficult to perform, read the example below. It may help you when examining your job.

Mary and her Section

Mary supervises four sales assistants who work with her in a branch of a national chain store. They work in the toiletries section.

What information do Mary's staff require to do their jobs? They need to know about the products, price of all stock, how to operate the cash register, deal with various methods of payment, how to deal with customer enquiries and complaints. They should know the location of other sections. The manager does not need to know any more than that Mary's section is running smoothly and meeting its sales targets.

Your peers may be interested only if their section is adjacent, or their products related, to yours. They may need to know whether your staff are specialists in any particular product in case of customer enquiry.

6.3 Types of Information

As a supervisor you should recognise two types of information.

• *Operating information* – used to do the job; it contains the details, quantity, finish, stanards, etc., and is usually long-term, and often general in nature.

- *Control information* – used to make sure that the job is going according to plan, the targets are being met, etc. This information is often collected for someone else. Control information is often short-term and specific in nature.

These two types of information have different uses, and can be contained in the same message; do not forget their different uses. Because control information is often used by others, we overlook its significance. This is the cause of much hassle in some organisations. Your staff may want to know why they are required to supply certain data which seems pointless to them. You will find the distinction between operating and control information a useful one.

Here are examples of control information and operating information:

Example 1 Sales assistants need to know the price of products and restock levels. Their managers need to know rate of sales and ratios of sales of these products.

Example 2 Machinists need to know the data necessary to manufacture component parts, when to start and when they are to be completed. Supervisors in a machine shop need to know which parts are holding up assembly, material availability and manufacturing data.

Exercise 6.1

In Examples 1 and 2 above, can you identify the control information and the operating information? (Five minutes.)

Activity

Can you determine whether the information you handle at work is operating information, control information or both? (Ten minutes.)

6.4 Supervisory Applications of Communication

We have looked at the 'big picture', the firm and communication in general, and you have examined your role in passing on information at work. Now we move on to the more specific applications, where you as a supervisor are associated with *communication*.

Exercise 6.2

List five key activities which rely on effective communication for results at work. (Five minutes.)

Supervisors are communicating in different ways throughout their working day, using both formal and informal systems. In this section we take the most important applications and examine them:

- Giving work instructions.
- Training staff.
- Meetings.
- Interviewing.

Giving work instructions

You will have been doing this regularly since becoming a supervisor. You have probably done it intuitively and may wonder why we are bothering to consider such a routine task. But the *results you achieve* are dependent on *doing this effectively*. Let us examine this application systematically. We will use John, a supervisor, and Mary, one of his staff, to illustrate this application of communication.

Mary produced the perfect job, using John's job instructions. For this to happen, Mary needed (1) the appropriate resources, (2) her skill and knowledge and (3) John's instructions.

If Mary followed the instructions exactly and easily, we must say that John gave excellent instructions. (Note, we did say Mary needed them.) Mary's skill and knowledge combined with the appropriate resources to give ideal performance. This could have occurred only after good instruction. Mary received these instructions, so she is part of the system. The instruction was more than a message, it was an example of communication in practice.

Let us consider closely the three elements identified above:

- *The appropriate resources* – John made sure that these were available and made the completion of the job possible, at the right time.
- *Mary's skill and experience* – do not forget that part of Mary's skill was in 'getting the message', apart from getting the job right.
- *The instructions* – there had to be a message. For it to be effective it had to be well received. This means that the instruction process was conducted in the right atmosphere. The supervisor had planned the job, organised the resources and made things happen to his plan.

Notice how *planning*, *organising* and *controlling* keep cropping up.

Exercise 6.3

List the factors a supervisor has to consider at the planning stage of work instruction. Which factor do you consider the most important? (Five minutes.)

Self-check

What might have been the consequences of the supervisor giving the same instruction to Mary's father? (He works on the same section as Mary.)

The only relevant additional information you have is (1) the job will be done by a man and (2) the job will be done by someone older. Could either of these factors alter the final result? (Ten minutes.)

They might. Only the supervisor on the spot, knowing the job, and the man, could judge. You may have said:

- The job might take longer.
- It might not be to the same standard.
- The supervisor may have to exercise more control while the job was being done.
- If Mary's dad was as skilled and knowledgeable as she – no change.

Summarising this section on work organisation, we recommend you consider these points whenever you give work instructions:

- Consider the person under instruction and their *needs*.
- Plan and organise *in advance*.
- Create the right atmosphere for *receptive communication*.
- *Instruct clearly*; identify any snags you may foresee.
- Check *feedback* for understanding.
- *Monitor* to ensure all is under control
- *Modify instruction* if necessary.

Training

Having examined work instruction, we can move on to training, another application of communication, as it follows the same process, with emphasis on different areas. The trainee will require more *attention* than an operator; the task will need to be *demonstrated* and *explained* in more detail.

The trainee should be encouraged to demonstrate both *understanding* and the *practical skills* needed for the satisfactory completion of the task. To ensure this, the trainer should establish what knowledge and skills are required for a particular task, and this can be used for checking the trainee's skill and knowledge, before and after training.

The trainee should be at, or above, the minimum standard before training is started. The task should be broken down into parts that can be easily understood and mastered in a systematic, logical manner before the whole task is attempted. So the trainer should be patient, work at the trainee's pace and understand the trainee's needs. The trainer is often in a position to decide when training takes place (as opposed to job instruction); this allows some flexibility.

Meetings

- 'What a waste of time, it's always the same – yak, yak, yak and nothing ever gets done . . . '
- 'What was all that about? Does anyone know what's going on . . . ?'
- 'How was I supposed to know they would want data at the meeting? I thought we were only planning in case . . . '

Have you heard comments like these made after some meetings you have attended? We have, and we sympathise with you. Meetings which produce comments like these are ineffective, demotivating and waste a lot of time. We are going to examine the process of meetings so that you can get more from them and run them more effectively.

What is a meeting? A meeting is a gathering of two or more people for a specific purpose. The legal definition of a meeting is 'an assembly of people for a lawful purpose' (*Sharp* v. *Dawes* 1876).

Reasons for meetings   These are some reasons for holding meetings:

- Because they are required by law or by the rules.
- To inform.
- To collect information.
- To decide on a course of action.
- To solve problems.
- To get commitment to a particular course of action.
- To allow for representation by groups.
- Combinations of the above reasons.

Your role at meetings   If you attend a lot of meetings then you probably have different roles at different meetings as a member, representative, specialist or organiser. We examine each in turn.

- *Member*   At work you may attend union meetings. If you are not on the committee you attend as a member. You attend when and where the meetings are held and discuss whatever is on the agenda. The agenda for the meeting will be drawn up by the committee at a previous meeting. You do not have a lot of control over the subjects discussed at a meeting if you are there as a member – you are an *individual* and responsible only for yourself.

- *Representative*   You may be on the committee of your local sports club with a particular responsibility – perhaps representing the football section. Your role would be to represent your section as a member of the committee. You are no longer speaking for yourself. To represent your section you must *know their views*, and be able to put their message across.

Activity

As a supervisor, you attend meetings at work. Do you represent your section? How do you find out the views of your section? (Five minutes.)

The answer to the first question will depend on your style of supervision; your answer should have been 'yes'. The second question was also checking your style of management; you may have answered it by saying 'by consultation'. Good.

There are many ways of consulting. Do you consult your section:

- As a section all together?
- In small groups?
- By selecting a few?
- Individually?

If you do not consult in any way, please read the section on leadership style in Chapter 3.

The answer you gave to the second question in the last activity gives us a chance to look at an organisational reason for holding meetings. If you try to tell everyone everything, you can't do much work. You would always be at meetings. Huge assemblies are difficult to control and, if everyone gets a chance to speak, meetings would go on for ever.

The problem of meeting size forces organisations to use *small groups* to make decisions. Small groups can work better because control is easier, and theoretically everyone can have their say. Representatives, who really speak for and protect the interests of their section, department or union in meetings, are the nearest we can get to a democratic ideal.

- *Specialist*   There are many meetings at which a 'specialist' is invited to give information, judge and evaluate information, advise, or guide the meeting. You may have to play this role. At a meeting to decide the best way to install a piece of machinery, the plant engineer would be there to provide specialist information about lifting, moving and installing the machinery. The other members would be there to find out how this would affect their sections, keep in touch and help with advice.
- *Organiser*   The last role we will consider is that of the organiser – the person who initiates the meeting. The duties of this role are discussed later in the chapter.

Self-check

List the main differences between being the organiser and a member, representative or specialist. (Five minutes.)

The main differences are that the organiser has to set the objective, date, time and location. He is in charge and directs. In the other roles you are guided by the organiser.

Types of meeting

- *Formal meetings*   Formal meetings have written rules and procedures. The term 'formal' here does not describe the behaviour at the meeting; it implies the formality of the *procedure*. The chairperson at a formal meeting would invite you as a member to 'speak' to the meeting. You would address your remarks to 'the chair'. 'Motions' are proposed by someone, and need to be seconded by another (member) before they can be discussed. Once a motion has been debated and a vote taken, it either 'falls' or 'is carried'. All very formal, but sometimes unproductive. Formal meetings have appointed or elected officers with special roles – e.g., chairperson, secretary and treasurer.
- *Informal meetings*   These need rules as much as formal meetings do. These procedures may be unwritten, but should be observed to ensure that results are achieved. More *self-discipline* is necessary than at formal meetings, because the lack of rules makes for heavier reliance on roles. Informal meetings need skilful chairing to make them effective. There is no need for special titles as long as the functions of chairperson and secretary, if necessary, are performed.

The role of chairperson or 'leader of the meeting' is vital to the success of any meeting. Often the leadership is challenged; this is normal behaviour in a group, provided too much time is not wasted on these power struggles. Groups need a leader for direction. Informal meetings often have secretaries who jot notes, as a record of what was decided; these can be referred to but are not usually 'published'.

Activity

Consider this question: which are more effective – formal or informal meetings? (Three minutes.)

The success of a meeting doesn't depend on the type of meeting. It depends on:

- The *people present* and how they behave.
- The *atmosphere* in which the meeting is held.
- The *effectiveness* of the communication.
- The *size* of the meeting

Try to involve people more, tell them what is going on. Give them an incentive for attending meetings. Invite them to meetings. Give them a chance to speak when they are there. The best way to get people to attending meetings is by *making meetings effective* and taking decisions, solving problems, passing on information quickly and efficiently, using all the skills and experience of those present.

Exercise 6.4

1 How many of the roles outlined above do you play at the different meetings you attend? (Two minutes.)
2 How does the role you play alter your involvement at the meeting? (Ten minutes.)

Guidance for members, representatives and specialists   Here are some guidelines which we hope will make you more effective at meetings.

1 Before the meeting   Before attending any meeting ask yourself these three questions:

1 Do I know what this meeting is *about*?
2 Do I know *why* I am attending?
3 Do I know *what is expected of me*?

Your answers should be 'yes' to all three. Once you know what it is about, why you are going and what you have to do when you are there, you can decide what preparation is necessary.

Your answers may persuade you to miss the meeting! If you cannot answer the questions yourself, get answers before the meeting and attend only those meetings which you need to or want to attend. Warn the meeting of absence, and if you feel like it tell them why! Persuade your boss to leave you out of meetings that don't concern you. If everyone who was invited to a meeting did this you would have smaller, better-informed and more effective meetings.

The answers to questions 1, 2 and 3 will provide you with the following information:

1 will give you either an *agenda* for a formal meeting or a list of topics if the meeting is informal;
2 will *define* your role;
3. will give you the chance to collect the information necessary to play an *effective part* in the meeting.

2 During the meeting During the meeting, if the process of communication is effectively followed, those present should know what is going on: information should flow, decisions should be made and objectives met.

At meetings you may be a 'sender' one moment and a 'receiver' the next – these roles require different skills. Improving your listening skills will increase your value to any meeting you attend, provided you then use the information you have received.

Remember you may be there to *get your message across*. The way you put your message will always affect the way it is received. Remember your *objective* – you want your message to be accepted. Watch your tone and style; do not get aggressive; persuade, do not bully; do not lose your cool.

There is no point in going to a meeting with a closed mind, so be prepared to be persuaded by logical argument. You may not get the point if you do not *listen*. New facts that emerge from a discussion, or even new understanding, may alter your message. (If you do not want to listen to other points of view, why bother to attend meetings? Submit your message in advance and get on with things you consider to be more urgent.)

It may be hard work, but do try to listen, not just to the words; get hold of the undercurrents, watch for all the *non-verbal communication* that is being displayed: 'read between the words'.

You want the other people there to listen to you. You can switch them off with emotive words and by blinding them with facts. Make your case stronger with diagrams, figures and visual aids.

Activity

The next time you attend a meeting:

1 Practise your listening skills.
2 Jot down the main points of an argument.

After the meeting, check your version of the meeting with those of others present, and evaluate how accurate your view was.

3 After the meeting Meetings are held for many reasons. When you think a meeting has been a waste of time, try to figure out *why it failed*. Check this out with others present. You may have missed something they gained from the meeting. You may get a clearer picture of other people's aims and objectives. Some people attend meetings for their own ends – they like to get on their soap box and develop their pet theory. Or they just like the sound of their own voice.

Others are not always quite so apparent, and are often said to be discussing items on the 'hidden agenda'. 'Budgets 1985' may be what you think you are discussing, while someone may really be trying to get more micro-computers for their departmental use. They are using the meeting for their own aims.

Do tell people what happened at the meeting.

Activity

Consider any recent meetings you attended. Try to identify any 'hidden agenda' items that were raised. (Ten minutes.)

Using the 'hidden agenda' is a useful way of getting things into debates and discussions. Your understanding of what is going on around you will increase your involvement, interest and effectiveness.

Guidance for the meeting organiser Some of you chair meetings in the course of your job. To conclude this section on meetings as an application of communication, we describe the activities the organiser undertakes in the three phases before, during and after a meeting.

1 Before the meeting The organiser of an informal meeting or the chairperson for a formal meeting will have to consider three main areas beforehand: planning; the agenda; preparation.

- **Planning** The organiser decides what the *objective* of the meeting is. What does he want to happen? Is there a real objective, or is it that we always have a meeting every month/week/term? What type of meeting is it? Consultative, informative, decisive or just routine? At this stage people must be considered. Who should attend and why? Who else needs to know about the meeting?
- **The agenda** Make sure the agenda goes out on time and contains all the items you intend to discuss, in the right order with the right amount of detail to *signal your intentions* to those who are to attend.

  At a meeting one of the authors of this book attended recently, 'production targets' were on the agenda. As he was not sure exactly what the intention was, he phoned the chairman, who explained that we would be looking at *next year's* production targets. The meeting was chaotic – the majority of those present came prepared to defend their failure to meet the previous month's targets, or to prove that next month's targets could have been met if . . . The meeting was adjourned so that we could return prepared to deal with next year's targets. A lot of time was wasted, a lot of unnecessary work was done and all to no avail!

  The date, location, time and, if possible, the duration should be included in the agenda. A list of those invited is often helpful. Ask for confirmation of attendance. If possible, ensure that anyone who cannot attend will pass their opinions, data and feelings to you so that they can be presented to the meeting.

Activity

Examine the agenda for any meeting you have attended. (Readers who do not attend formal meetings may turn to the end of the chapter for an example agenda they can use for this activity.) Compare it with the notes above. What did you learn from this comparison?

You may have found nothing wrong! Some common faults are:
1 No idea who else is attending.
2 Agenda arrives too late for preparation.

3 Items in the wrong order for logical decisions. Sometimes all the work done early on is wasted because of decisions taken later in the meeting.

4 Subjects not detailed enough for preparation.

• **Preparation** Naturally the preparation for any meeting will depend on the points about *planning* and the *agenda* discussed above. Ensure the *venue* is available. Ensure that *your whereabouts* are known by those who might need to contact you in an emergency. Do not assume that everyone knows about your meeting! Delegate someone to look after your work in your absence.

2 During the meeting So far we have looked at the preparation needed to set up a meeting. Now we look at some of the essential requirements for the successful running of a meeting. Here is a list of the points you should concentrate on if you want to make your meetings more successful.

• Be punctual. Start on time.
• Observe the rules of communication.
• Listen carefully.
• Summarise often to check understanding.
• Maintain team spirit.
• Protect the underdog.
• Be fair, firm and maintain discipline.
• Steer the discussion if people wander from the point.
• Encourage participation.
• Learn how to control conflict, go for 'win–win' outcomes in cases of conflict (see Chapter 3).
• Practise observing what is going on in the group (see Chapter 3).

3 One problem area examined Meetings fail for many reasons. Sometimes no conclusion is reached, or no solution found, because of a combination of bad chairing and lack of disciplined meeting skill. People at these meetings move the discussion in various directions and the meeting gets confused. There are too many topics under consideration at one time. This problem can be overcome by someone, usually the chairperson, summarising the situation and identifying the number and nature of the problems under discussion. The next step is to arrange these *in priority* (a mini agenda!) and then deal with them *in order*.

Once this has been done, proceed through the steps listed below:

1 Make your case, or let the person concerned make his case.

2 Collect relevant evidence, information, opinions.

3 Discuss the evidence, information and opinions as fully as needed; give everyone a chance to contribute.

4 Arrive at a solution, or solutions.

5 Evaluate the implications of these solutions.

6 Agree on a solution.

7 Decide on action necessary to implement the decision.

8 Move on to the next problem.

4 After the meeting   Often it is after a meeting that we can assess its effectiveness. This is the time to check that your objectives were achieved or, if not, why not. Now is the time to discover why things went the way they did – remember to look at your successes as well as your failures!

Check that all actions agreed at the meeting have been allocated to an individual and that these actions are being progressed. Make sure that a record of the meeting is made for future reference (these records are called 'minutes') and distributed. Where necessary report to the appropriate authority the outcome of the meeting.

5 Behaviour at meetings   Behaviour at meetings follows the same pattern as that in groups, provided the size of the meeting is no larger than twelve (see Chapter 3 on groups). In larger meetings, unless they are carefully controlled, you can often identify the number of small factions making up the whole.

Exercise 6.5

List the skills which must be exercised by people

1 attending meetings;
2 chairing meetings.

(Five minutes.)

Interviews

An interview is a meeting of two or more people with a specific objective. Interviews are held for a variety of reasons. While the specific purpose of each interview is different, they all have four distinct phases. The initial letter of each phase spells the word WASP to help you remember them.

Welcome: the interviewer is *put at ease*.

Acquire: give the interviewee a chance to give you the information you require.

Supply: give the interviewee all the information needed (for him to judge *what you are offering*).

Part: close the interview – making sure the interviewee knows *what is expected*. Agree the action to be taken.

Most interviews have some sort of follow-up to ensure that actions agreed then take place later. Remember the preparation steps for any effective communication. Refer to the *process of communication* (Chapter 5) and remember the work needed before the transmission stage.

Interviews are no different from other forms of communication. Prepare for every interview in a logical, systematic way.

Activity

List the communication skills that you think an interviewer should have. (Ten minutes.)

Because interviewing is an application of communication, you should have listed all the skills needed for *oral communication*. You may have added some or all of the following skills which are particularly useful when interviewing.

- The ability to *persuade*.
- The ability to *analyse and evaluate information coming in* rapidly.
- The ability to *listen*.
- The ability to 'steer' an interview in a *chosen direction*.
- The ability to *summarise* to establish what is being discussed.
- The ability to *get information*.
- The ability to *interpret non-verbal feedback*.
- The ability to *record accurately* what is said.

Does this list look familiar? It should do; it is similar to the list you drew up for exercise 6.5!

Activity

In what ways are meetings and interviews similar? (Two minutes.)

Interviews are small meetings with the interviewer in the role of organiser or chairperson, and the interviewee as a member or specialist. Some interviews have panels of interviewers – they appoint their own chairperson. The rest of the panel are there as specialist or representatives.

Some obstacles to good interviewing, and their remedies   All too often, interviews go wrong and we don't achieve our objectives; we feel uncomfortable with the outcome and unsure of what we expected. Here are some of the obstacles which might be responsible, and their appropriate remedies.

Obstacle	*Remedy*
Too little time allowed	Make time before an interview to *prepare for it*. Allow enough time for the interview itself.
Distrust	*Instil confidence* in the interviewee. Be assertive. Be honest, sincere and fair. Build a reputation which makes people trust you.
Fault finding	Be *positive in your criticisms*, concentrate on solutions instead of 'nit-picking' and destructive references to past behaviour.
Rigidity of view	Be *flexible*. Listen to the other person's point of view.
Your attitude	Always approach an interview with the belief that you can arrive at a mutually satisfactory outcome. While this may not always be the outcome, it will certainly help you if you believe that there is a win–win solution (see Chapter 3 on conflict).

Types of interview and their purpose   We are going to examine a range of six different types of interviews in this section:

- *Selection* – interviews are carried out to select the right person for your requirements.
- *Induction* – follows to introduce the successful candidate to his new environment, job and workmates.
- *Coaching* – a form of informal training which you can use to encourage your staff to solve their problems.
- *Counselling* – used when staff have problems.
- *Disciplinary* – interviews held to bring about a change in behaviour.
- *Terminal* – interviews held to allow staff leaving the company to 'get it off their chest'.

1 Selection   The purpose of any selection interview is to choose the *right person for the job in question*, or to select someone who shows *potential for more senior posts*. Interviews may not represent the ideal method of selecting staff. For one thing, you will not know whether you have selected wisely until long after the interview. The period you have to wait will depend on the job in question – the lower the level of the job, the quicker you will discover how good you were with your selection. Be clear what you are trying to achieve by the interview, and how you intend to do it.

Interviewing requires many skills which develop only with practice. Be careful that you are not being subjective in your judgements; try to be *objective* wherever possible. An example may illustrate the point. If you interview a long-haired applicant, you may be put off by the length of his hair; you may associate long hair with untidiness, dirt or laziness. This is a subjective judgement – another interviewer may not be affected by hair length in the same way.

Subjective misjudgement is sometimes called the 'halo and horn' effect. This is how it works. We meet someone neatly dressed and well spoken and from this we assume that they are all things good; they will be reliable, honest, hard-working, etc. We are blinded by their halo. Conversely, on meeting a roughly spoken scruffy individual we decide they will be unreliable, careless and lazy. We only see their horns. This problem needs to be overcome, since we could so easily overlook first-class candidates for vital posts because we have not been objective.

One way of being objective is to try to use a *scale of measurement* that will give the same result no matter who uses it. This is not easy to do, but is worth the effort involved if you are to improve as a selector of staff.

There are many interview plans available to help you to be more objective. Let us examine that of J. M. Fraser. If you do a lot of selection interviewing we recommend you read his book, *Employment Interviewing* (Macdonald & Evans, 5th edn, 1978).For the purposes of selection interviewing, he sets out the following five personal qualities for consideration.

- *Impact on others*, or the kind of response an individual's appearance, speech and manner call out from others.
- *Qualification and experience*, or the knowledge and skills different types of work require. (This area is broken down into three subsections: (a) general education, (b) vocational training, (c) work experience.)
- *Innate abilities*, or how quickly and accurately an individual's mind works.
- *Motivation*, or the kind of work that appeals to the individual, and how much effort he is prepared to apply to it.

- *Emotional adjustment,* or the amount of stress the individual will experience while involved in working with other people.

These five qualities are each divided into five grades which range from the bottom 10 per cent of the population (E), through the next 20 per cent (D), the middle 40 per cent (C), the upper 20 per cent (B) and, last, the top 10 per cent (A) of the population. Each grade is clearly described; and using this information a picture of the 'ideal' candidate can be built up. This can be used as the basis for your selection – your *standard.*

Selection is now reduced to answering two questions: Do I know exactly what I want? And will I recognise it when I see it? You still require the skills of interviewing to check that your interviewee is in the appropriate grade.

You were probably surprised when we said that interviews were similar to meetings. When you interview someone for a job they seldom realise that it's they who have written the agenda for their 'meeting' in their letter of application! If your personnel department do the shortlisting, then you are playing the role of 'specialist'.

Activity

How can you tell if you are a good selection interviewer? (Five minutes.)

If the candidate you selected comes up to your expectation in performance then you may be a good interviewer, or you may be lucky.

Keep a record of how you rated each candidate you interviewed at interview and after an appropriate time has passed. If you consistently predict performance to match their interview rating, you are a good interviewer. If your judgements are wrong, examine your criteria for selection and get them right. You can't afford to make mistakes.

2 Induction   Can you remember your first day in your present job? Were you anxious, confused, lost, afraid? Most of us were, and that is why an induction interview is so important. A good induction interview starts workers on the right lines, making them feel part of an organised team, and reassuring them that they were expected and that some trouble was taken on their behalf to make them feel at home.

Common sense, planning and a little organisation before the event are all that are needed.

- Have you made time to show the new worker around?
- Have you informed his workmates and your manager?
- Are you clear exactly what job has been allocated to the new worker?
- Has your new worker any disabilities?
- Will you be able to recognise your new employee – or, better still, be able to make a good impression by knowing his name?
- Is there a work place for him?
- Is there somewhere to hang his coat?
- Does he know where to park, eat, draw his wages, go to the loos and the hundred-and-one other details that he's worrying about?

Don't forget to leave time to answer questions, and try to *listen* to what is being asked. Listen for the anxiety behind the question and sort it out as quickly as possible.

Do you have a check list of what should be covered in an induction, or do you work from memory?

Have you 'appointed' someone as a 'friend' to look after the new worker?

Activity

If you do not use a check list, draw one up for future use and amend it to include those new questions that the latest newcomer asked. (Ten minutes.)

Reassure the new worker that he's welcome; the sooner this person is integrated into the team, the sooner you can leave him to get on with the job. Anxious workers do not work effectively – happy workers do. Make everyone on your section feel wanted, part of a team. Tell them your goals and expectations right from the start. Explain the standards you have set and why.

Coaching   Part of a supervisor's job is to train his staff. This may be done in a variety of ways, both formal and informal. Coaching is one way to train your staff informally.

Coaching consists of getting people to accept that *they* own a problem and then encouraging them to solve the problem for themselves. This does not mean that the supervisor should not help the problem owner; but it does mean that the supervisor must not *impose* solutions on the problem owner.

Often your staff come to you with their work problems and you immediately offer solutions. This behaviour has two effects on the staff:

they expect you to solve their problems; and as a result they become conditioned to this situation and your workload is increased. *They do not develop* and you do not really get to know how they think. If you get your staff to recognise that they can solve their own problems, and that is what they are being paid to do, then you are well on the way to getting them to do just that.

Wouldn't your job become easier if people came to you with a number of solutions to a problem and asked your advice on their relative merits? This would be preferable to them appearing with the problem and the expectation that you will sort it out.

The following example may help you to understand how coaching works:

Mary and Janet

Mary is an office supervisor and Janet is one of her section leaders over a pool of four typists and two shorthand typists who serve seven offices. Mary has four other section leaders beside Janet.

Janet: 'Mary, Pat (one of the shorthand typists) hasn't turned up for work and Joan (typist) is still away with flu. What shall I do?'

Mary: 'Thanks for telling me, Jan. How much work have you got on today?'

Janet: 'Oh, mostly routine stuff except for those meetings.'

Mary: 'Which meetings do you mean?'

Janet: 'A production meeting where they need a secretary, and the sales managers' meeting. Oh yes, then there's a bit of work for old Thingy in Research.'

Mary: 'How do you plan to cover these three, and cope with the routine work?'

Janet: 'That's what I am here for, Mary, I'm asking for help.'

Mary: 'When are these meetings, and how long will they last?'

Janet: 'The production meeting starts at 10.30 and usually goes on till 12.30. The sales managers start at 1.30 and they take about one hour.'

Mary: 'O.K. How about Ross in Research; when did he want to dictate his letters?'

Janet: 'He doesn't mind – any time we want.'

Mary: 'So what's your problem, Jan?'

Janet: 'Well, Pat hasn't turned up for work and she usually does the sales managers, and Betty (a typist) wanted the afternoon off so we will be short on typing.'

Mary: 'Who else could do the sales managers' meeting?'

Janet: 'Oh, anyone I suppose. OK, I'll put Jill on to that and she can do the production meeting as well.'

Mary: 'Great. How about Ross, who can handle his work?'

Janet: 'Come to think of it, we can do him after the sales meeting . . . '

Mary: 'So, there's still the routine shorthand and typing – how do you think your girls will cope?'

Janet: 'I'll have another look at it and sort out the priorities and we'll do what we can.'

Mary: 'Let me know if you have any snags once you have looked at the priorities and we can decide what to do. O.K? Let me know then whether Betty is having the afternoon off.'

Janet: 'I'll have a chat with her and see how desperate it is for this afternoon – perhaps once she knows what's going on . . . '

Mary could so easily have solved Janet's problems, thereby taking them away from her. This way, Janet has really examined her own problems and, more to the point, solved them herself. Coaching takes up time, but has the advantage of developing the individual and including them in the decision making process. Many supervisors have difficulty in allowing others to make decisions. Bite the bullet – let your staff have a go. Warn them of any snags that you can see; encourage them to work things out themselves and then to discuss their ideas with you. This way they *grow with the job*, and in discussion with them, you learn informally how much they know; this provides you with an ideal opportunity to fill in the gaps in their knowledge. (See 'delegation', Chapter 8.)

Exercise 6.6

Could you use coaching in your job? What are the steps in coaching? How do staff benefit from coaching? (Ten minutes.)

---

4 Counselling Supervisors are often seen by their staff as having the answers to all problems. This is another example of the halo effect. 'My supervisor is a damn good bloke – he will know what to do . . . ' As a result you are often involved in counselling interviews where *your* advice or counsel is sought. This aspect of a supervisor's job can have a spin-off on other areas of his work. It improves individual motivation, helps to build the team and often the quality of the work itself improves in an atmosphere where people are prepared to ask for, and take advice.

Remember what we stated in Chapter 4 on listening: listen carefully to what people have to say; it is surprising how bad we are at listening. If you listen you will frequently get past the apparent causes of a lot of problems and deeper into the real core of the problems. Often your merely listening is enough to help a person solve their problems.

In cases where your advice is sought in areas beyond your knowledge or experience, do not be afraid to admit you do not know. You may still be able to help by finding out where information can be obtained, and you may pass the problem on to the relevant expert without destroying the relationship already built. Problems related to drugs, drink, marriage and domestic affairs may all come your way. Be conscious of the trust placed in you and always check how confidential the information is. Create an atmosphere in which your staff come to you with their problems, knowing that you won't gossip and betray their trust. However, be careful to avoid taking the problem from them; they must always remain the problem owner if it is their problem.

Activity

One of your staff has recently become moody, irritable and slow. What would you do:

1 ask him directly what is wrong and if you can help; or
2 ask his mates?

(Two minutes.)

Wherever possible, you should go directly to the person concerned; only if this fails, and the consequences of this person's behaviour are serious, should you approach others to try to discover the cause. Most people dislike being talked about behind their back. Often the real picture is blurred or distorted by the interpretation of others, who may not know all the facts (see Chapter 3 on groups).

5 Disciplinary   Disciplinary interviews are one of the least popular tasks that a supervisor has to perform. In this section we are looking at them in the context of communication; later in Chapter 8 we will look at their legal aspects.

Activity

Write down what you consider to be the objective of a disciplinary interview. (Ten minutes.)

You may have written one of these answers:

- To give the culprit a verbal hammering.
- To explain company policy, etc., then to clobber the culprit.
- To find out what is causing the problem.
- To produce a change in behaviour.
- To let the culprit know who is the boss.
- To do what your boss says has to be done in these cases.

Be very clear in your mind why you are conducting this interview. Your main objective should be *to bring about a change in attitude* and then – and only then – to take any necessary action. Often these two are reversed, so that managers clobber the person concerned, then tell them why, then ask if there is any reason for their conduct!

Here is a model procedure for disciplinary interviews:

1 *Prepare for the interview*. Collect facts, data, etc. Provide a location and make sure you will not be disturbed.
2 Let the interviewee say his piece. Listen to the information he supplies. *Decide if this alters your view*.
3 *Put your side of the story*. Explain the implications to the team and the company. Set out the statutory background if relevant. Do not get bogged down in unnecessary detail, e.g. 'You were ten minutes late', 'No, it was only eight minutes', when the issue is *lateness*.
4 Identify the *cause* of the problem. Do not confuse symptoms with complaints.
5 *Work together towards a solution*.
6 *Agree the solution*.
7 *Keep a record of relevant data*. If you are recording information during the interview, tell the interviewee.
8 Arrange a *follow-up interview* if it is necessary.

If at any stage the discussion becomes too heated to be rational, either have a break or adjourn the interview until you have cooled off. This could save you making a fool of yourself, or prevent the interviewee saying something that might be better left unsaid.

6 Terminal   In any healthy organisation there is bound to be a coming and going of staff. To gain benefit from an employee's departure, you should seek out their views on the organisation in a terminal interview. These interviews can yield valuable information which workers who are staying on may not care to reveal.

Would it be to your advantage to know the real reason why someone is leaving your company? Could you and the company benefit from a worker's opinion on safety, house-keeping, supervision, promotion prospects, work methods, etc.? Should you try to find out what might induce the worker to stay on?

The terminal interview is a formal way in which to end a professional association, and the information obtained from it could benefit you as an individual, your team and, indeed, the company as a whole.

Activity

List the questions you would ask at a terminal interview of an employee aged forty-five who has worked at your firm for ten years. (Ten minutes.)

With ten years' service you could learn a lot. Your questions could include:

- Why are you going?
- Are you going to another job?
- What did you like/dislike about working here?
- What changes would you have liked to see made?
- Where are you going and why?

6.5 Written Communication Applications

Report writing
Report writing is the most demanding of all written work. If you can do this, you can cope more easily with any of the other applications you use as a supervisor. A report is a document which records facts and opinions, observations, calculations, conclusions and may contain a recommendation.

Objective   Before you write any report you should be crystal clear in your own mind WHY are you writing your report. (In other words what is your *objective*?) What do you want to *happen* once your report is read?

Activity

Why am I writing this report?
Jot down your reasons. (Five minutes.)

You may have any number of reasons written down:

- Because I *have* to.

- Because I *want* to.
- Because I wish to *improve* some aspect of my job and the report will make this improvement more likely to happen.
- Because it will provide *evidence*.
- or allow *comparisons* to be made,
- or analyse *facts*,
- or collect *opinions*,
- or recommend *solutions*,
- or record what is *actually* happening.

Do you think the third example given above is a better reason for writing a report than the other two? If you answer *yes*, then ask yourself: *why*? You should come to the conclusion that you will be better motivated to write a report if you think you are going to get something changed, improved – or, perhaps, even stopped. If you are better motivated you should, as a result, work more effectively. To make the best of any report you must decide *who best can make things happen*, and the report should be aimed at them.

The receiver   All reports are aimed at a receiver (or receivers), and therefore should be written in such a way as to *maximise their impact*. If the receiver is an expert you will not need to go into the same details that a less experienced reader would need. If there are receivers of differing levels of expertise and knowledge you will have to word your report so as to include all the readers – this is much more difficult, and what you include and how you write your report will govern its understanding, subsequent acceptance and implementation.

Reasons for reports
Reports are written for various reasons, for example

- To *record* – accident reports, machine performance.
- To *inform* – accident reports, progress reports.
- To provide *evidence* on which decisions can be made – accident reports, test reports.
- To *persuade* – accident reports, report on machinery performance to encourage replacement.

Activity

Explain why 'accident reports' appear in the above list four times. (Five minutes.)

Reports have many uses. Let us trace the route an accident report may have to take:

1 An accident report is often completed soon after the accident occurred. This would be a *record*.
2 A copy of this may be sent to another department, a higher authority or an insurance company. The purpose could be to *inform* them of the accident.
3 If there was a court case or a safety enquiry, then this report could be used as *evidence* of fact.
4 This report could also be used to *persuade* someone to take action.

Types of report

Reports, like meetings, may be *formal* or *informal*. The choice between these types will often be governed by the subject, the use to which it may be put and its intended reader. Some organisations insist on formal report, at all times, others leave the choice to the individual.

If you are in any doubt, use the type of report which you judge will meet your objectives; reports going outside your section and being used by others should be typed. All reports should be well laid out and clearly presented.

Formal reports   Formal reports usually follow the structure outlinedbelow. Where possible we have given a very brief example of what a report might contain.

- **Title**   The title should be clearly worded and reflect the *contents of the report*.

Example
'Car-parking' is ambigous as a title if a report is about a specific car park and the problems of overcrowding. A better title would be 'Bridge Lane car park utilisation'.

- **Terms of reference**   These must state exactly what was required, who the author is, and who requested or authorised the report. These should be set out in a *formal style*, quoting instructions, names and titles.

> *Example*
> 'I was instructed by the Works Committee to:
>
> 1 examine the present parking arrangements at Bridge Lane.
> 2 evaluate alternative sites if necessary, and
> 3 recommend solutions.
>
> From J. Bloggs, Services Manager.'

- **Summary**:   This section may be necessary for long, complex reports and gives the reader a *brief preview of the report*.
- **Contents**:   Even a short report should have a list of the main headings and subheadings, and where they can be found (e.g. page/para/nos). This can be at the front or back of the report.
- **Introduction**:   This section *sets the scene for the report* and explains why the report is necessary, and often identifies the problem that the report should resolve. It may include a brief historical background, definitio of terms, description of constraints on the investigation, etc. and may also show why you decided on a particular procedure.
- **Procedure or investigation**:   This would outline how the report was tackled, the methods used, locations, dates and the people concerned. This tells the reader how, where and who *collected the material* for the report.

> *Example*
> 'The Bridge Lane car park was observed at random intervals over four working weeks and data recorded. A random cross-section of staff (16) using the car park was interviewed and their comments noted. The information was analysed and tabulated. The following alternative sites were examined for possible use: Cannon Close and George Street.'

- **Findings**:   Lists of facts and their sources are recorded in this section in logical, sequential order, or in the most appropriate manner. *No options are stated*. This section would contain tables of data, analysis, dates, times, numbers, etc. This is the main BODY of the report and contains EVIDENCE.

Because you will, inevitably, have more information than you can use, carefully select the material you include in your FINDINGS. Take care to PRESENT it in the best possible way to maximise its impact on the receiver. Why not use key words, underlining, CAPITALS and other layout devices to highlight the thrust of your message.

- **Analysis and conclusions**:   The findings are analysed and opinions stated. Arguments are put forward and eventually *conclusions are drawn* from the analysis of the findings.

    Do take care to be analytical! Use the evidence you have collected and prove a case. Do not pull solutions out of thin air. Your conclusions must flow from your findings and be validly derived.

Example
'As a result of the analysis of my findings I came to the following conclusions:

1 The Bridge Lane car park was frequently overcrowded
2 This problem will last until January 1989
3 Adequate parking was available at George Street.'

- **Recommendations**:   (If required by the terms of reference)   The logical step after coming to a conclusion is to follow it through to a *recommendation*.

Example
'From my conclusions I am able to recommend that:

1 We commence negotiations to retain 25 spaces in the George Street car park for staff from B workroom (see Appendeix III).
2 Until the additional parking places are available we transport staff from Bellview Estate at our cost.
3 All staff are informed of your decision as soon as possible.

Signed J. Bloggs
        Services Manager.'

- **Signature status and date**:   These tie it all up neatly so that the author can be identified, and is prepared by virtue of his signature to be *accountable for the report*.
- **Appendices**:   Often these contain samples of data, supplementary material, calculations, diagrams and supporting evidence that may be required, and they must be referred to in the body of the report. However, only include *necessary detail*. Do not pad your report with junk!

Informal reports   Informal reports could follow the same structure leading from title through the stages outlined above but using a less formal style. Provided a report is clear, concise, well argued, has sufficient evidence and is well presented it *should* achieve the desired result, even if it does not follow exactly the structure detailed above.

You have been introduced to Report writing, and how it will be valuable to check your understanding of this important communication process.

Activity

Skim quickly the proposed structure of a formal report outlined above, and try to establish the *purpose* of each section: e.g. TITLE – tells the reader what to expect. (Five minutes.)

Hints on report writing

- Make the layout *easy to read* by varying paragraph sizes, using plenty of subheadings, and breaking up blocks of text with tables or idented lists.
- Wherever possible *quantify your findings* – e.g. 'on six occasions (Jan 7, 9, 12 and Feb 3, 5, 7)' is much more effective than just saying 'it often happened'.
- *Cross-refer* to pages, paras and appendices when necessary.
- A *contents page* is useful both to you and your reader – do put one in your report. It may also sometimes be appropriate to give further references.
- Do not go overboard on numbering (para 2.3 (iv) (a) etc!). But be able to *refer to a detail*.
- *Provide proof* whenever possible.

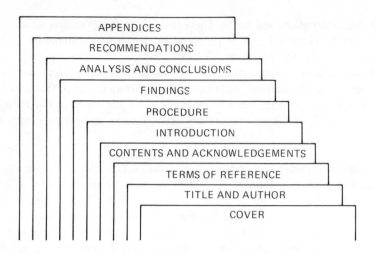

Fig 6.1   *Format and content of a report*

- If you quote other people's work or statements do tell the reader the *source of your information*. Be sure to acknowledge any help you have received.
- *Plan and organise* your material *before* you start writing. Start with a blank page for each section of your report. On each page note the headings and content. Check the flow across the pages. Do you need more proof, or can you remove some without detracting from the report? It is much easier at this stage than when you have pages of words!
- Always consider the *impact on people*, the *efficiency* of the report and the *cost* to implement your recommendations.

Figure 6.1 lays out the format and content of a report in diagrammatic form.

By now you should be clear about the structure of a report and what each section *does*.

- The *terms of reference* dictate what you should do.
- The *procedure* will govern your findings – their quality and validity.
- Your *analysis* of these will be helped by your presentation and lead to a logical *conclusion*.
- This should be supported by *evidence* collected to lead naturally to a *recommendation* which ties up with the terms of reference (see Figure 6.2).

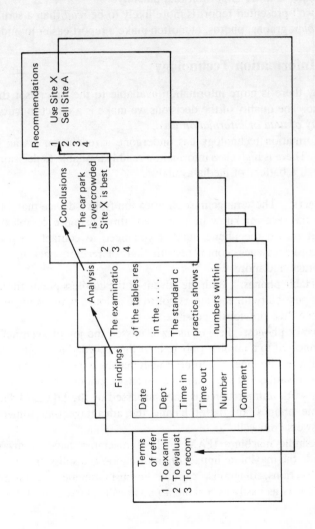

Fig 6.2 *Report writing sequence*

Finally, ask yourself the question: *Will this report make the things happen that you want to happen*? ie has it met your original objectives? *Remember*:

1 *Quality* is more important that *quantity*.
2 A well presented report is more likely to be *read* than a scruffy one.
3 *Tables*, graphs, photos, etc. often make a report easier to understand.

6.6 Information Technology

Today there is more information available to the supervisor than ever before. The quality of the decisions we make is a direct function of the *quality of data or information used*.

Information technology has undergone a revolution in the last few years. There is high class information readily available to decisionmakers through a battery of media available:

- **Pagers**:   These range in sophisitication from a device that 'bleeps' to let the receiver know he is needed, through more complex gadgets that record the phone number you need to contact, to packs that record messages, complete with time of receipt, back up facilities, storage and more.
- **Portable phones**:   With the advent of the cordless phone there is now the possibility for the supervisor to be in touch with events in a larger arena than previously possible.
- **Answer phones**:   Few of us have missed the joy of eventually being connected to a number only to hear the recorded message invite us to talk after the tone . . . Infuriating it may be but efficient it certainly is. The advantage of switching over to answerphone while we get on with our work uninterrupted is only surpassed by the DIVERT facility on some phones, the latter having the advantage that someone else answers your call!
- **Facsimile machines (FAX)**:   These machines have in my opinion made the maximum impact on information transmission. Documents, instructions, diagrams, can all be instantaneously transmitted to receivers as easily as making a phone call. Do you use FAX in your job?

6.7 Computer Applications

Supervisors today use computers or their output as a matter of course. Many have their own terminals through which they keep in touch with the rest of their organisation (or others if they are 'networked' or interactive). Most of you will have access to microcomputers with access to programmes such as spreadsheets, databases, and wordprocessing in general and specific or 'dedicated' packages associated with your job.

Peripherals: VDUs

When connected to computers, VDUs (visual display units) give us a means of seeing what is being computed. These displays may be in the form of written texts, calculations or diagrams.

Inputting data

There are numerous ways to input data into computers:

Keyboards: These look like a typewriter but may be a bit more complex to operate and are probably the most common way of 'talking' to a computer.

Light-pens: These are the magic wands that read *barcodes* and other coded information.

Printers: Driven by computers, printers can be used to produce memos, records, letters, diagrams, calculations or graphs.

Computers can be interconnected to other computers to pass on or collect information. Machines and processes can be controlled to predetermined standards by computers.

A lot of people are wary of computers because they are not familiar with them, nor do they trust or understand them. Soon computers will be accepted as a powerful tool to be used to improve our efficiency in everyday life.

Future uses of computers

Imagine a VDU, printer and terminal in place of every telephone in your company. All these 'communication centres' would be connected to a computer with access to all the information needed to run your company. At any time you could interrogate the computer and find out the *immediate availability* of all the *resources* of the company.

Decision making Because of the power and speed of the computers, you could carry out complex processes instantly – e.g. the comparison of various solutions to a given problem could be examined against the variables of time, cost and resources. You could select the *ideal solution*, and the computer would put your decision into action. Materials, machines and workers would be allocated, the appropriate people informed and records immediately updated.

Planning, organising and controlling   In Chapter 4 we looked at these basic supervisory functions, and saw control as a system with inputs, outputs and feedback.

If for all three of these functions the computer had mathematical rules governing their interdependence, it could rapidly calculate and compare a variety of combinations of data to identify the *ideal solution* to any given problem. This is not possible using present manual systems, because of the time needed for the calculations.

The outputs from planning would be the inputs to organising, and all new information about the processes would be inputted into the control system, which would provide the information to control the process automatically. These three processes would become a routine function once all data was available to the computer.

Communication   Located around your work place would be a number of interconnected communication centres, which would be externally linked to other computers at your suppliers, customers, banks and transporters, to mention but a few outlets.

Because these centres would produce letters, memos and diagrams, you would send and receive information to anyone in or outside the company at will. The computers would talk to each other, make decisions in your interests and report back to you. Letters, memos, notices and instructions would be produced at the receiver's terminal.

Noticeboards   These would be replaced by communication centres which anyone could interrogate to retrieve current or historic data.

Selection   Because all relevant information was already stored in the computer, the specific requirements for every job would be available. If applicants for a job recorded their personal details on a computer form, selection interviewing – as we know it – would become obsolete. Applicants' data could be checked against the requirement for the job, and a decision instantly made regarding suitability for a vacancy.

Training   Training is another area in which the computer could be useful. The trainee could be monitored by the computer while doing a standard routine, and skill levels recorded.The computer would then determine what training was required and how best this could be done for each of the skills needed for the job, and for the trainee concerned. During training, which would be on a simulator, the trainee would use computer-aided learning packages and be brought up to the desired standard of performance as efficiently as electronically possible.

Activity

Examine a noticeboard at work. Decide:

1 What should be currently displayed.
2 How you would store all the information that is not displayed, but which someone might need urgently at any time.

(Ten minutes.)

---

1 Your answer will depend on the purpose of the particular board you chose, and your work.
2 You have thought about the needs of your reader in deciding what is currently required. This leads you into identifying what might be needed and does not need to be displayed, before you decide how you will store it. It would be much easier if we did not have to make this decision. Could we store all information just in case it was required? How much space would we need?

If we kept all the data anyone might need, we would have to satisfy the following requirements:

● Space to store the data.
● A system to store, file, find, replace and update the data.
● Time to find the data, extract it and replace it in the right place.

You will have difficulty satisfying these requirements with a manual system. The computer would treat this as a routine task and deal with with an enquiry immediately.

Having taken this look into the future, we leave you to consider the implications of computers on your own lives.

6.8 Summary: Communication in Action

In this chapter, we looked at the applications of communication, the various types and systems used. We examined the giving of work instructions, the process of making meetings and interviews effective and how to write a report. Finally we looked at computers, a modern form of communication, which will soon allow us much more time to concentrate on the real issues of supervising people. Until this happens you will have to rely on the available techniques and make the best of them.

Chapter 7 deals with the techniques you will have to use until computers play all the roles we have forecast.

Sample Agendas

(For use with activity on p. ○○○.)

CORHAM WIND & WATERSAIL

to: DW   Date: 8.10.199–
    TC   Time: 10.30 a.m.
    KH   Location: Boardroom
    MLS
    JMH
    etc.

Six-monthly planning meeting

A G E N D A

1 Minutes of last meeting

2 Matters arising from minutes:

3 Sales forecast

4 Production for next period

5 The market:

6 Any other business:

J. Seeley
MD

Once you have completed the activity on p. ○○○, compare this agenda
with the modified agenda below. Notice these improvements:

- Initials and departments. Ken Porter, newcomer.
- Duration of meeting.
- More details to allow members preparation.
- Logical flow of subjects.
- (J M H) is warned that he may need figures for 3.

CORHAM WIND & WATERSAIL

to: D W (marketing) Date: 8.10.199–
    T C (sales) Time: 10.30–13.30
    K H (production) Location: Boardroom
    M L S (distribution)
    J M H (finance)
    C B (production)
    F R (costing)
    Ken Porter (computers)

Six-monthly planning meeting

REVISED AGENDA

1 Minutes of last meeting

2 Matters arising from minutes:
  a. Letter from America:
    Our position on Surfboard concession
  b. Investigation into supply hold-ups:
    D W to report
  c. News:
    i. New orders
    ii. Patents approved
    iii. Sales analysis

3 Sales forecast
  K. H. wants to replace the LM70s with G84s (JMH)

4 Distribution:
  M.L.S. problems with existing contract
  Options for consideration

5 The market:
  TC to explain his findings after his UK and Continental tour

6 Sales forecases:
  To predict sales for Jan–Jul.
  TC to outline marketing strategy.
  KH to provide capacity data
  Discussion.

7 Production: Jan–Jul.
  To arrange production from sales forecast

8 Any other business:
  Car parking.

J. Seeley
MD

7 Techniques to Help the Supervisor

The supervisor's job is to get the job done by effectively organising and controlling the work of the section. Chapter 4 expands on this aspect of supervisory work in detail and refers to techniques which can help. This chapter outlines the most useful of these techniques and gives opportunities for practice and guidance on the possible application to your own work.

On completion of the chapter, you should be able to explain what the techniques are about and how to use them in your own job. We have limited our coverage to those which can be used in the day-to-day work of supervisors, and not included any which are best used by specialists. Most of the techniques involve use of numbers, and we start with a look at handling simple numerical information. If you can handle numbers you might skip the first section, but work through the self-checks to be sure.

The chapter briefly covers:

- Handling information.
- Techniques for analysing work.
- Planning methods.

7.1 Handling Information

With computers becoming more integrated into business activity at the working level, supervisors should know something about the way information is processed and have some understanding of the language of numbers. Managers talk in terms of percentage increases, rates of growth, overhead margins and similar jargon. For this reason, and because some of the techniques involve the use of numbers, we start this section by illustrating certain basic methods of calculation that all supervisors should be familiar with. You should not be frightened to talk the language of numbers. What happened to Tom Stranks is a typical example.

Activity

Tom Stranks was called into his manager's office to discuss the running of the section.

'I'm worried about the amount of overtime that you are allowing your people to work, Tom. You know that your budget for the year is 2,400 overtime hours and here we are at the end of the fifth month and you are already 23 per cent over. Can you account for it?'

Calculate the excess overtime hours.

List three reasons which might explain why Tom has exceeded his budget. (Five minutes.)

If the annual overtime budget is 2,400 hours, the monthly budget is $2,400 \div 12 = 200$ hours per month. By the end of the fifth month, if Tom was strictly on budget his section would have worked $5 \times 200 = 1,000$ hours. The manager says he is 23 per cent over.

23% of 1,000 is $(23 \div 100) \times 1,000 = 230$. So the section has worked 230 hours over budget. Tom's total overtime worked so far is $1,000 + 230 = 1,230$ hours. Here are some reasons why this may have occurred:

- The work in the section is seasonal.
- There has been a higher rate of work than was assumed when the budget was drawn up.
- There has been a high rate of sickness covered by extra overtime working.
- The budget was totally unrealistic in the first place.

You will have experienced situations like this where you are called to account and you have to be very quick on your feet so that you can answer the case being put.

Percentages

Percentages are used in many applications of managerial control. You have only to look through your daily paper to see them quoted in many references, often in a most misleading way. To see how information can be presented in a misleading manner you should read Darrell Huff, *How to Lie with Statistics* (Penguin Books).

Uses of percentages take three forms:

- One value is expressed as a percentage of something else: £55 as a percentage of £375 is $(55 \div 375) \times 100 = 14.6\%$.
- An increase in a value is expressed as a percentage increase: the price is up from £48 to £53, an increase of $(5 \div 48) \times 100 = 10.4\%$.

- A decrease in a value is expressed as a percentage decrease: sales last month were £2,885 but they are down to £2,400, a decrease of $(485 \div 2,885) \times 100 = 16.8\%$.

In working with percentages there are three simple points to remember. We will go through these with some opportunities to practise. If percentages are easy for you then skip this section, but do not kid yourself, try the exercises first!

The three points to remember with percentages are:

- *per cent* means 'per hundred', so 23% means 23 per hundred, or $23 \div 100$ as a fraction;
- *of* means 'multiply', so 23% of 198 is $(23 \div 100) \times 198 = 45.5$;
- *of what*? must be asked to be clear as to the base figure of the calculation. When the manager says to Tom, 'You are 23 per cent over budget,' Tom must be clear as to what the actual budgeted figures are.

In all numerical work that you do, use a calculator if you can. But always estimate the answer before operating the machine, as a check.

Exercise 7.1

1 You have been awarded a pay rise of 5%. If your monthly pay is now £450 what will your new monthly pay be?

2 'Expenditure on consumables last period was £2,850; this period it's £3,250; what is that as a percentage increase?'

3 'This item is now produced for a works cost of £3.75. That represents an 8% increase on the previous value.' What was the previous figure?

(Ten minutes.)

Ratios and proportions

These are often used in a similar way to percentages. A *ratio* shows the relationship between the parts which add up to a whole. A *proportion* is a measure of the size of a part relative to the size of the whole.

For example, in Tom Stranks's department he has 24 operators for whom he is responsible. There are 20 men and 4 women. So what is the relationship between the number of men and the number of women employees?

We say that the ratio of men to women is 20 to 4 or, as it is normally written: the ratio of men to women is 20 : 4 (the colon : indicates a ratio). Since the ratios are simplied down to the simplest numbers, the final statement of this would be that the ratio of men to women is 5 : 1.

Self-check

Because of a change in work load, four of Tom's men are transferred to another department. What is the ratio of men to women in his department now? (Two minutes.)

There will now be 16 men to 4 women, so the ratio will be 16 : 4, or simply 4 : 1.

Now consider expressing these figures as a proportion – that is, the measure of the size of one part relative to the size of the whole. What proportion of Tom's department is women? There are 4 women and with the new arrangement the whole department totals 20, so the proportion of women is $4 \div 20 = \frac{1}{5}$, and by similar logic the proportion of men in the department is $\frac{4}{5}$.

Notice that in quoting a ratio we show the relationship between the two parts of the whole, part 1 : part 2, whereas in proportions, we relate each part to the whole, part 1 ÷ whole, and everything is reduced to simplest possible figures.

Exercise 7.2

1 Dave has a section of 15 staff which has a ratio of 3 : 2 between women and men. How many of each does he surpervise?
2 Helen supervises the audio and photographic section of a retail department store. Takings last month were £4,500 on audio and £6,000 on photographic. What is the ratio of photographic to audio sales? What proportion of total sales is earned by audio? What is this as a percentage?
3 The company accountant Stewart Wales has the problem of sharing out ('apportioning' he calls it) the cost of running the canteen between departments X, Y and Z. He decides to do it in proportion to the numbers who work in each department. The total monthly cost of the canteen is £3,000 and the numbers working in the departments are 50 (dept X), 30 (dept Y), 70 (dept Z). What cost should he allocate to each department when calculating overheads?

(Fifteen minutes.)

Averages

Many uses of numbers involve handling groups of numbers, and to explain these it is not sufficient to work with percentages and ratios alone. We have to express a *typical value* which reasonably represents a set of values. This is called the *average*.

Consider the case of the small company Brackets Ltd where the employees are making a case to the manager for a wage increase. Business has been good and the employees feel that their earnings are a bit 'below average'. The manager replies that earnings in Brackets are above those in the locality, as the average earnings in the company stand at £516 per month. The men cannot counter this argument but feel that there is something wrong. The supervisor finds out that the earnings are as follows for the people who work for the company (monthly gross earnings are quoted in £s) for each of twelve staff: 400, 400, 200, 800, 400, 400, 500, 400, 400, 1500, 400, 400.

So the manager is quite correct in his statement. What he has done is add up all the figures, which give a total earnings for the month of £6,200, and divide by the number of employees, giving an average of £6,200 ÷ 12 = £516. Do you think that this is the most representative value?

What we really need is a figure which best represents the group of numbers which are the earnings for each person in the firm. There are three types of 'average' in use and we must distinguish between them:

- *Arithmetic mean* – this is the one that the manager has used; it is the sum of all the values divided by the number of values in the set. This is the most frequently used method of finding the representative value of a set of numbers.
- *Median* – this is the middle value of a series when it is arranged in ascending order.
- *Mode* – this is the value that occurs most frequently in the set of values (the most fashionable number).

Going back to the earnings at Brackets Ltd, we can work out the three different forms.

Arithmetic   mean = (200 + 400 + 400 + 400 + 400 + 400 + 400 + 400 + 400 + 500 + 800 + 1500) ÷ 12 = £516.

Median is the middle value of the series: 200, 400, 400, 400, 400, 400, 400, 400, 400, 500, 800, 1500. As we have two middle values we take the average, which is £400.

Mode is the value which occurs most frequently = £400.

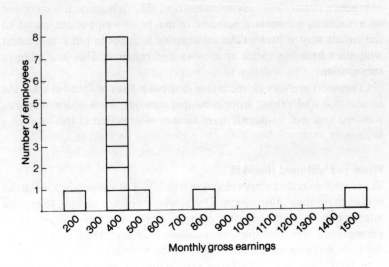

Fig 7.1 *Brackets Ltd: distribution of earnings*

You will now see that people use the 'average' which best suits their argument. In this case the manager has included the two managers' salaries, which lift the average, whereas a negotiator for the staff would use the median, which best represents the staff earnings. In general the mean is the most likely average to be used.

The picture is shown more clearly if we draw the numbers graphically, as in Figure 7.1.

Exercise 7.3

The ages of the staff at Brackets Ltd are as follows: 46, 38, 44, 54, 36, 23, 48, 18, 46, 48, 52, 46.

Calculate the arithmetic mean, median and mode of the ages.

Draw a diagram similar to the one show in Figure 7.1. You will have to lay out a scale which groups into intervals 15–19, 20–24, 25–29 and so on.

7.2 Presenting Information

We are all bombarded by information every day. Sales information, government information and media information floods out, often presented in a way that gives only a partial view of the truth. Much information made available to managers is presented in a way that is easy to produce rather than easy to understand. This is because it is compiled on a machine, a computer perhaps, or maybe on a typewriter, on which the easiest way to present the information is either to put it in the text with the words, or to list it in rows and columns. This is a table of information.

Computers are very clever at churning out masses of data but you have to search it and extract from tabulated data just *what information you require*. You will frequently have to face information in the form of a table.

When you will need this skill

There are two main circumstances in which you as a supervisor will need skill in presenting information. One is where you are seeking to explain information to staff, and the other is where you have to report to management. For example, the manager may say: 'Look into this, get the facts and give me a short report on the situation.'

In both cases it may be more satisfactory to present the numerical information in the form of a diagram. Many supervisors find it useful to use drawings or diagrams which present the information clearly, simply and with greater impact than a table can do.

Methods of presentation

We will now consider three methods of presenting information:

- Tables.
- Pie charts and bar charts.
- Graphs, where one variable is related to another.

Tables   A table is an array of numbers presented in an orderly fashion in rows and columns.

Activity

List five tabulations that you are likely to see in the next few days. (Five minutes.)

There are many possibilities:

- a bus or train timetable;
- your company analysis of performance;
- sales information in advertisements;

- the schedule of work duties in your department;
- the football pool results;
- the display of prices in your local pub.

Tables are widely used for presenting large quantities of information, partly because of the ease of production and also because they are capable of setting out much information in a relatively small space. Pictorial methods are often much clearer, but carry much less information. It is not possible to lay down a set of rules about the layout of a table of figures because there are so many different uses. Above all the information must be set out in a way which makes it easy for the reader to find the information required.

When drawing up a table of figures keep in mind the following:

- Tables are constructed in *columns* (vertical) and *rows* (horizontal). Think carefully about which information you are going to put on which *axis*.
- Columns and rows should have *headings* to tell the reader what the information is. It should be possible to read all headings without turning the document.
- The shape of the tabulation must be designed to *fit the document into which it is going*.
- *Proper use of space* within the tabulation is the best way to help the reader. Space should be used to separate groups of information, and to help to lead the reader's eye along the paths that separate the sections of a complicated tabulation.
- *Heavier type or underlining* can be used to differentiate between section of the table.

If a table is thought to be too complicated, then some form of diagram can be used.

Pie charts and bar charts   These charts are well named because a pie chart looks like a pie cut into a number of portions, and a bar chart looks likea lot of bars all standing together. Pie charts are good for showing the proportions of the parts of something; they present the information as portions of a circle and so are sometimes called circle charts.

Consider this: 'In the survey it was found that the average family spent £160 on regular expenses, which was allocated so that the largest share went on food (£56), with entertainment (£32) and taxes and savings (£32) the next largest, with rent (£24), and clothes (£16) making up the rest.'

Self-check

Calculate the percentage share of each item and draw this information up as a simple table. (Fifteen minutes.)

Allocation of the average family expenditure

Item	Expenditure (£)	Percentage (%)
Food	56	35
Taxes and Savings	32	20
Entertainment	32	20
Rent	24	15
Clothes	16	10
Totals	160	100

To represent this information as a pie chart, we have to work out the angles at the centre of the pie by proportion. Since the angle of the circle is 360° this represents the total expenditure of £160 and all the other values are related to that. For example, the angle for food is $56 \div 160 \times 360° = 126°$; so we draw the circle to a size appropriate to our layout, draw a line as our base line, and then using a protractor mark off 126° (see Figure 7.2).

Fig 7.2 *Pie chart: first construction*

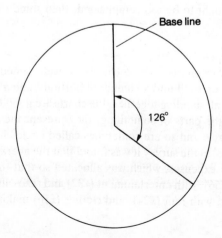

We now do this again for the other items.

Exercise 7.4

Work out the other angles for the other items and draw the lines to construct the pie chart. (Ten minutes.)

Bar charts do not require the same sort of calculation, since the proportions can be simply marked off on a scale. They can be drawn horizontal (bar chart) or vertical (column chart) as you judge best (see Figure 7.3).

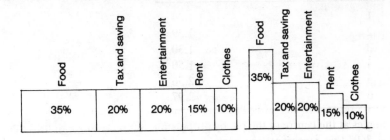

Fig 7.3 *Bar charts: allocation of average family expenditure*

You will see many forms of bar chart used in newspapers or on television. They are more useful than pie charts, which although they show proportions very well, are not much good for anything else. Bar charts can be used to show *trends* and compare one set of information with another, and they are quite simple to prepare. As with the pie chart, care must be taken in drawing the bar chart. There must be a clear title telling the user what it is about, the scale must be clearly indicated, and you must avoid cramming too much information on to one chart. If you have a lot of information to display, it may be better to put it on to two separate charts for increased clarity.

Graphs   These are widely used in many applications, some of them in a very specialised way by scientists and engineers. In their simplest form they can be very useful to the supervisor because they show the *relation between two things that vary*, for example how sales have varied over a period of time. A graph is drawn on two axes for which appropriate scales have to be chosen, and the values of each set of data are plotted and then connected up to form a curve. To see how this is done, let us imagine that you have been asked to explain the changes in unemployment over a six year period. You have looked up some figures which are tabulated like this:

Unemployment (United Kingdom)

Year	Number in millions
1	1.34
2	1.39
3	1.30
4	1.50
5	2.56
6	2.97

To draw the graph mark out the scales (called *axes*) with time going across the bottom and the scale for the number of unemployed up the side. The 'dependent variable', as it is called, is always plotted on the *vertical* axis, and in this case the unemployed number varies with the year, so we plot it as shown.

The size of the scale is chosen to suit the layout, but keep in mind the reader and try to avoid a layout which requires the reader to turn the document sideways. The choice of scale will also affect the apparent steepness of the graph. Having drawn the axes, we carefully plot each point and connect them up to show the trend, as in Figure 7.4.

By choosing different scales it is possible to alter the appearance of the graph to make it either flatter or steeper according to what you are trying to show. If you wanted to exaggerate the climb in unemployment you could extend the vertical scale, as shown in Figure 7.5.

If you wanted to play down the rise in unemployment you could use a compressed vertical scale and extend the time scale to give an apparently slower rate of increase. Look for examples of this sort of manipulation of graphs that you see in the newspapers and magazines. Sales advertising is full of the steep 'gee whiz' type of graph, as Darrell Huff calls it in *How to Lie with Statistics*.

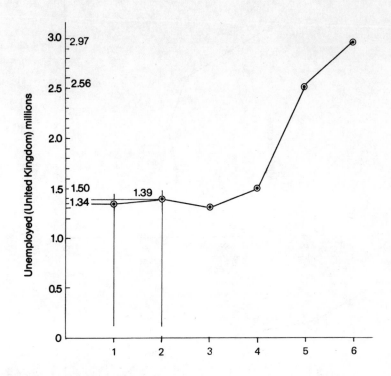

Fig 7.4   *Unemployment: United Kingdom*

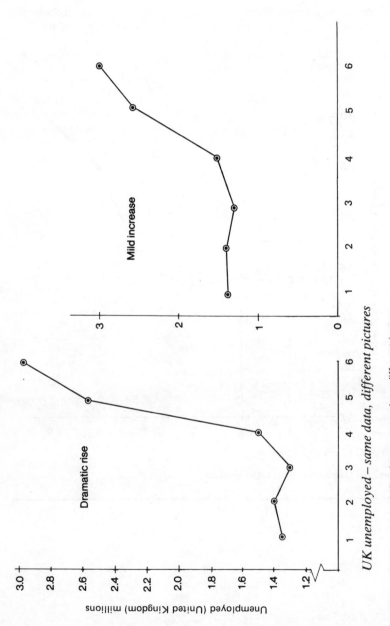

Fig 7.5 *Unemployment: United Kingdom – same data, different image*

Exercise 7.5

In Tom Stranks's department the demand for product X varies considerably throughout the year. This causes problems for Tom. The figures are:

Jan.	Feb.	Mar.	Apr.	May	Jun.	Jul.	Aug.	Sep.	Oct.	Nov.	Dec.
110	140	180	190	185	170	175	195	210	170	120	95

Tom wants to make a case to his manager to see if this variation in load can be smoothed out, to help with planning the work of the department. Tom will want to use an expanded scale which will make the variation more pronounced.

Draw a graph which will help him to make the point. If you use squared paper it will be easier. (Fifteen minutes.)

Summary: presenting information

That concludes our examination of the methods of presenting information. Here are the key points:

Tabulations

- good for presenting a lot of information;
- easy to produce on standard machines;
- leave the reader to do all the work.

Pie charts

- good for showing proportions;
- unsuitable for a lot of information.

Bar charts

- easy to draw;
- good for a wide range of uses;
- somewhat limited in the information they can show.

Graphs

- show how one variable changes with another;
- easy to prepare but easily distorted.

7.3 **Techniques for Analysing Work**

In Chapter 4, on work organisation and planning, we referred to certain techniques which the supervisor can use in this crucial aspect of his or her work.

There are two reasons why you need to know about these techniques. One is that in organising work you need a keen eye for the methods by which the work is carried out, and must constantly search for ways to reduce costs, improve productivity and make life better for the people in the section. The other reason is that sometimes firms employ specialists for this purpose, often called 'work study' or 'O & M', or 'management services'. The work of your section may be examined by these specialists and their reports presented to management. You should know enough about the techniques to give the specialist the right information and to ensure that the specialist takes into full consideration the needs and the problems of your section. You should be able to look at the report confidently, and should be able to make sensible comments to ensure that no factors about the work of your section have been overlooked.

Work study techniques are the ones you are most likely to be affected by. They can be divided into two main areas:

- *method study* – which is concerned with finding a better way of doing things; and
- *work measurement* – which aims to measure the work content of a task so that a value expressed in time can be arrived at for planning and control purposes.

We will take each in turn, concentrating on those aspects which are most useful to you.

7.4 **Method Study**

In trying to find a better way of doing things, it is important to work in a systematic way and follow an orderly disciplined approach. Over the years, work study practitioners have evolved a procedure which provides this discipline. It does not mean that you can rely on the procedure to produce the improvement; you still have to apply your mind and think creatively, but it does avoid your jumping to conclusions.

The method study approach can be described as a six-step procedure:

- *Select* the task or problem to be studied and define what you are trying to achieve.
- *Record* the facts relating to the way in which the job is being done.

- *Examine* the recorded method in a critical way to expose the undesirable features of the present method.
- *Develop* a new and better method from this examination, building on the essential elements of the task and the needs of the worker.
- *Install* the new method, taking care to keep in mind that people do not like change, and explaining fully to those affected by the change.
- *Maintain* the new method by checking occasionally to make sure that the new method does not drift off the planned way.

This presentation gives an easily remembered sequence which can be worked through where there is a problem at the workplace. Method study can be applied to any physical work; in the factory, in the kitchen, on the farm, in the office. The six-step description sounds a bit mechanical, as if the procedure will automatically produce good results, but you know that solving problems is not all that easy, and often you have to retrace your steps in an investigation. To show this more flexible nature of method study, a different way of presenting the procedure has been worked out showing it more as a problem-solving routine, as in Figure 7.6.

Fig 7.6   *Method study procedure as a problem solving routine*

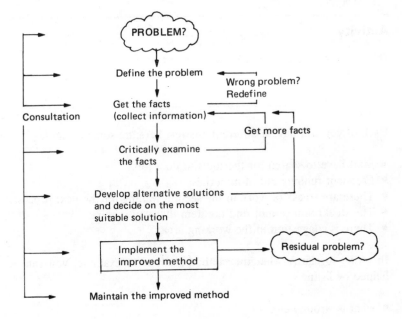

Self-check

List the six stages in the method study procedure, giving a brief explanation of each stage. What is the benefit of such a procedure likely to be to the supervisor? (Ten minutes.)

The six stages are: select; record; examine; develop; install; maintain. The procedure provides a discipline to prevent jumping to conclusions.

If we now consider each stage in turn we can see what is involved and show how you can use the procedure in everyday circumstances. We can call this 'do-it-yourself method study'.

The 'select' stage The difficulty of this stage is knowing exactly what to concentrate on. All of us feel that there are things at work that need improving but that they are usually someone else's responsibility. If you are seeking to improve things in your own section, it is best to start with something that *you can actually change*, rather than get frustrated to achieve something that can be done only by your managers. How will you know what to tackle? There will be *symptoms* that show that something is in need of investigation.

Only the staff in the section or their supervisor really know what the problems are:

Activity

Think of the problems in your department at work. List five symptoms which indicate to you the need for a study of the methods that are in use. (Ten minutes.)

Each of you will have a different answer; here are some examples:

- Staff have to search for the tools to do a job.
- Frequent running out of materials.
- There are stacks of work in the section waiting for the next process.
- The stockroom cannot find the item that you require.
- There is congestion in the working area.

In trying to clarify what the method study is to examine, you can be helped by listing:

- what is wrong *now*;

- what you see as the *problem*;
- what is to be *achieved*;
- an estimate of *likely success*.

Once you start looking you will probably find that the difficulty will be of deciding where to start – that is, unless you are so complacent that you can find nothing wrong to start with. If this is the case and you really do want to know, invite a friend or colleague to take a critical look around. There is nothing like a fresh eyes to see things that the resident takes for granted. If, as is most likely the case, there are several things that might need attention, you have the problem of deciding which of them to tackle. The factors to consider if you have to select are:

- Go for a problem that is *not too complicated*.
- Tackle something that is clearly *within your own authority*, and where you can actually change things. (All too often problems in your area will be the result of malorganisation at a higher level.)
- Go for something where you are *likely to get a good result*.

The 'record' stage　Here are the techniques which can help. The trained work study practitioner has a 'tool kit' of about sixteen different ways of recording what is actually going on, some of them quite complicated and not appropriate for this book. We are going to concentrate on three ways of recording work, each of which has its own usefulness. The purpose of the record stage is to collect all the facts that relate to the present method and to lay them out in a clear fashion for *analysis*.

1 Observing the work　This will require some observation of the work as it proceeds. Verify by direct observation wherever possible; do not take people's word for it – go and see for yourself. This may seem somewhat suspicious, but experience shows that this is a very powerful idea and will reveal many things. Look at the items which are being worked on; they always tell their story.

2 Techniques for recording work　Of all the ways of recording work for method study, three stand out as being of most useful for general purposes: the flow process chart; the flow diagram; and the multiple activity chart.

Flow process chart
'Flow process chart – a process chart setting out the sequence of the flow of a product or procedure by recording all events under review using the appropriate process chart symbols' – this and later definitions are taken

from British Standard 3138, *Terms Used in Work Study and Organisation and Methods*.

The process chart symbols referred to in the definition have been developed to help code the elements of the work that go to make up the whole task. These symbols are set out in Figure 7.7.

Using these symbols, a clear visual description of almost any sort of work can be drawn up.

Let us observe a manager at work. When he wants a letter prepared the sequence of events begins when he calls his secretary on the intercom; she goes from her desk to his office and takes a seat near his desk. He dictates the letter and she takes it down in shorthand. She then returns to her desk in the outer office and, if she has no more pressing work, types out the letter from her shorthand notes, with an envelope. When she has a batch of letters ready, or at the end of the day, she takes them into the manager for signing. The manager checks and signs the letters and the secretary prepares the letters for posting.

Fig 7.7   *Process chart construction: symbols to code the elements of work*

		Explanation
Operation	◯	Indicates the main steps in a process, method or procedure. Usually the part, material or product concerned is modified or changed during the operation
Transport	⇨	Indicates the movement of workers, materials or equipment from place to place.
Permanent storage	▽	Indicates a controlled storage in which material is received into or issued from a store under some form of authorisation.
Temporary storage or delay	D	Indicates a delay in the sequence of events or any object laid aside temporarily without record until required
Inspection	▢	Indicates an inspection for quality and/or check for quantity.

Let us now draw up a flow process chart for this work. The first thing we have to decide is, what are we going to chart? We have to choose whether to chart the person (in this case the secretary), or the material (in this case the letter), or in some cases the equipment (which is not appropriate in this example as there is no single piece of equipment involved).

Self-check

Which do you think would be the best to chart – the secretary or the letter?

The choice is not easy. To chart the secretary is simple enough but does not show the delay suffered by the letter while the secretary is doing other work; whereas to chart the letter is difficult because, in the early stages of the procedure, the letter exists only in the head of the manager.

Fig 7.8   *Flow process chart: preparation of a letter*

FLOW PROCESS CHART		MATERIAL TYPE *(Letter)*
OPERATION *Preparation of letter*		
DISTANCE (metres)	SYMBOL	DESCRIPTION
	①1	*Dictated to secretary and translated into shorthand notes*
6.5	⟨1	*Taken to secretary's office*
	D 1	*Wait for typing*
	②2	*Letter typed from shorthand*
	D 2	*Wait completion of other letters*
6.5	2⟩	*Taken by secretary to manager's office*
	▢3.1	*Letter checked and signed by manager*
6.5	⟨3	*Letter taken to secretary's office*
	④4	*Prepared for posting*

This matter of choice is not unusual, but the ovrriding question is, *what form of record best represents the work under study?* Here the chart of the letter seems slightly better. It looks as in Figure 7.8, with the main feature of all such charts – the process description – having the appropriate symbol alongside it, and the distance indicated where any transports occur. A very simple heading has been used.

Exercise 7.6

Draw your own version of the flow process chart taking the secretary as the subject. Interpret all the action from the view of what the secretary does. (Ten minutes.)

Flow diagram
If we need a record which shows the movements more clearly, we have to draw a *Flow Diagram* – 'a diagram or model, substantially to scale, which shows the locations of the activities carried out and the routes followed by workers, materials or equipment'.

To draw a flow diagram we need a drawing of the layout of the workplace and then we can plot over that the lines of movement. In the case of our office example, the layout looks as shown in Figure 7.9.

The actions already identified on the flow process chart are shown on the flow diagram, connected by the movement lines and thus giving an overall view of the work. In combination these two charts are most useful, and if you try to do a method study and are not sure how to record the work then start with a flow process chart and flow diagram.

Multiple activity chart
The third method of recording is most useful where there are several people or people and machines, working together. This is the *multiple activity chart* – 'a chart on which the activities of more than one subject (workers, materials or equipment) are each recorded on a common time scale to show their interrelationships'. Notice that this is the first of the charts to use a *time scale*, which means that you need to know how long each part of the work takes. The features of the chart are a time scale and columns in which the activities are marked out. Consider an example from the kitchen at home, in which we will chart the cooking of the Sunday dinner. We will assume that the cook has to cook roast lamb and two vegetables for four people; the operations are:

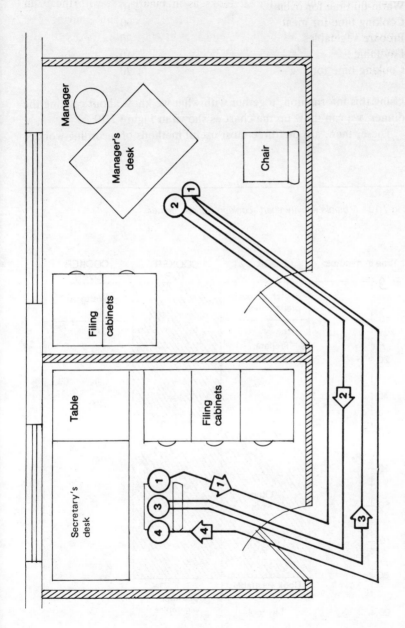

Fig 7.9   *Flow diagram: preparation of a letter*

Activity	Time in minutes
Warm-up time for oven	10
Cooking time for meat	90
Prepare vegetables	30
Lay table	10
Cooking time for veg	20

Using this information, together with what we know about cooking the dinner, we can draw up the chart as shown in Figure 7.10.

These, then, are the three most useful methods of recording work.

Fig 7.10   *Multiple activity chart: cooking Sunday dinner*

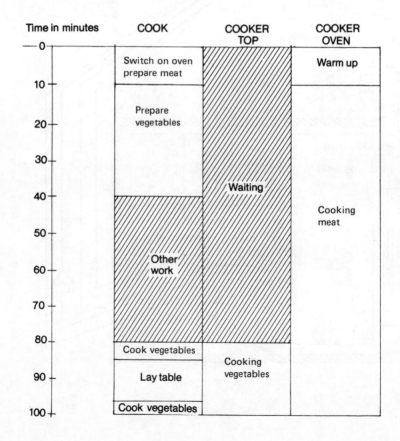

Exercise 7.7

What would be the most appropriate charting method for recording the following activities?

1 Filling shelves from the stockroom in a retail store.
2 The assembly sequence of an electric motor.
3 Two mechanics working together fit a new engine to a car.
4 A van driver making a delivery to a shop.

The 'examine' stage We now have the facts about the work. We can take these and study them in detail away from the distractions of the workplace. This stage is called 'examine'. The discipline of the method study procedure encourages us to take the recorded facts, look at them calmly and examine and question every aspect of the work that is being done. The critical examination procedure has been worked out to ensure that we do this thoroughly.

Certain points must be kept in mind:

- It is very easy to let preconception prevent the creation of new ideas. 'I have always done it that way' is not necessarily a reason for continuing to do so.
- If you have ideas that crop up in the early stages of the study, note them down at the time, but do not allow them to influence the end result until after the examination has been done.

Carry out the examination by using these questions on each part of the work:

	Primary	*Secondary*
Purpose	What is achieved?	What else could be done?
	Is it necessary? Why?	What should be done?
Place	Where is it done?	Where else could it be done?
	Why there?	Where should it be done?
Sequence	When is it done?	When else could it be done?
	Why then?	When should it be done?
Person	Who does it?	Who else could do it?
	Why that person?	Who should do it?
Means	How is it done?	How else could it be done?
	Why that way?	How should it be done?

Although this may seem an elaborate process, the main aim is to study the work carefully and challenge superficial explanations which are not basically sound.

Self-check

Go back to the record that we made for the work involved in typing a letter (Figure 7.8). For the process as a whole, check it through using the questions of the critical examination. Is there a better way? (Ten minutes.)

- *What is achieved*? Ideas in the manager's mind are prepared for sending to someone outside the company. *Why*? To achieve a specific objective of the manager's – only he know the details.
- *Where is it done*? In the manager's office. *Why*? To save the manager's time.
- *When is it done*? When the manager thinks of it. *Why*? So that he does not forget.
- *Who does it*? The manager and the secretary. *Why*? The manager has the idea and the secretary has the skill to prepare the letter.
- *How is it done*? The manager dictates, the secretary takes it in shorthand and then types the letter. *Why*? Because that is the company procedure.

You perhaps think that some of these explanations are too easy. The secondary question – what should be done? – brings out possibilities like 'telephone direct', 'use a dictating machine', 'learn shorthand himself'. From these will spring the new method.

The 'develop' stage   From the example of the letter we can see that the questions lead you towards a new method of indicating what improvements can be made. From the results obtained, you can develop the better method. You should now consider ideas for improvement that were thought of earlier or suggested by operators.

No rigid procedure can be laid down for this stage because the circumstances vary so much and the thought processes involved are largely intuitive. Try to cover every aspect of the work, the procedures, the layout of the workplace, the use of materials and the working conditions, so that a complete improvement is achieved.

Remember that when you are trying to find a new method you are likely to *change the working situation* for a number of people. Unless you are very considerate you will generate resentment in them.

Self-check

The supervisor in the assembly section had observed the difficulty that Elsie had in getting parts from the conveyor on her right, having to reach round to get each part. He decided that he could make her work easier by turning her bench at right angles to its original position (see below). She could then pick up the parts in front of her, do her part of the assembly and place it on the left of her bench so that Jean could pick it up. After he had installed the change he was amazed at Elsie's reaction. What do you think it was?

Look at Figure 7.11. The reaction was that Elsie was very upset and was quietly crying at her bench shortly after the changeover had been carried out. Her work was right off, both in quantity and in quality. When the supervisor talked to her about it he found that what had upset her was that she could no longer talk to Jean as she worked, and that all she could see was the conveyor in front of her with components apparently marching towards her all the time. We can see that the supervisor should have discussed the change with the operators first.

Remember, when developing a new and improved method you should try to think it through from the *operators' point of view*. Will the new method upset the work to such an extent that the overall effect is counter-productive and actually does more harm than good?

Fig 7.11   *Changing the working situation*

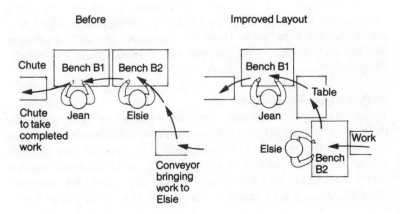

The 'install' and 'maintain' stages   Installing a new method will be easier if the *staff are involved*. If you impose change on the people in your section they will be much less likely to accept it willingly than if you involve them to some extent. You have to decide for yourself how much consultation is appropriate in your situation. This will depend on your own style, the type of work being done and the general climate in your organisation.

Activity

Suppose you are the supervisor of a small office section doing routine administrative work in a large organisation. On your staff there are a section leader, eight female clerical assistants and two juniors. From your experience of the work in the section you have formed some ideas to improve the layout. This will improve the flow of work and make it easier for people to get the files they need to do their job. The changes are quite easy to carry out since they only require movement of a few desks and filing cabinets.

How would you go about effecting the changeover? Write brief notes on your plan for the change. (Five minutes.)

The dilemma here is how to balance the need for direct action with the need to involve the staff and get their acceptance of the change. In putting this question to a number of people we have found a wide range of approaches. These range from those who would hold a series of meetings to explain and persuade the staff to agree to the changes, through to those who would come in over the weekend and change everything without previous explanation!

The best approach lies somewhere between the two. We would advocate discussing the ideas with the section leader to check that there are no unforeseen snags, and then explaining to the staff what the aim is and how you see the final layout. Then do it, giving help to adjust once the change has been made. There is no universal answer to a problem like this and the person on the spot has to decide. (See 'motivation', Chapter 3.)

Method studies by specialists

If method changes are devised from a study carried out by the specialists in the management services department of the organisation, then your role as the supervisor is rather different. You must be sure that the specialists have considered all normal conditions of the work and that they are not just going for efficiency without any thought for your staff. After all, the aim is to improve productivity. If we stick just to *labour productivity* then this can mean one of two things – either a higher output can be achieved from the same workforce, or if there is no demand for extra output then higher productivity means achieving the same output from a reduced workforce. It is this second meaning which worries worker representatives.

Maintaining the improved method is the final stage. After the difficulties of installation, when the new method has settled down, it is important to take a detailed look now and again to make sure that there is no drifting back to the old ways of doing things. It is worthwhile keeping some record, at the install stage, of the preferred method.

We have now completed our explanations of the method study procedure. We have dealt with it at some length because it can affect your whole approach to your work once you have practised the discipline. Above all, it develops a *critical eye for the way work is being carried out.* You never quite lose the questioning approach to methods, and find yourself asking (in your own mind), 'Why are they doing it like that? Surely there is a better way?'

7.5 Work Measurement

The other part of work study that we must look at now is work measurement, which aims to measure the work content of a task so that a *value expressed in time* can be arrived at for planning and control purposes.

We all carry out some form of work measurement even if we do not think of it in that way. When a householder goes out to do some work in his garden, he will plan to do certain things and judge approximately how long the different operations take. In this way he will make some estimate of what is possible in the time available to him. We all do this when we are planning things, and in estimating how long each part of the work is going to take we are using our experience to establish the time for each task.

In reality, the range of methods used to establish the time for a task is extensive, and methods vary from the very approximate to the very accurate. The approximate methods are used by everybody when planning work; the more accurate methods require properly trained specialists and must be left to them.

Methods of measuring

The methods used can be illustrated as in Figure 7.12.

It is essential that the values obtained are carefully maintained as measurement of work content, and in this respect the work study practitioner is the custodian of the time standards.

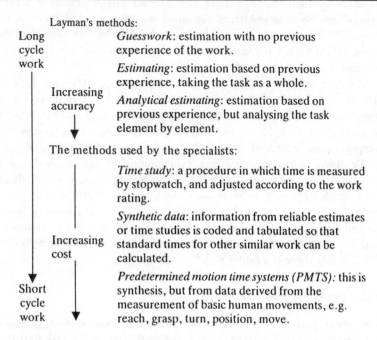

Fig 7.12   *Methods of measuring work*

Work is measured in terms of the time that it would take under certain conditions, and is expressed as a *standard time*. Never forget that it is a measure of *work content*, which will change if the method or materials or tools change. If the work in your section is measured and your staff work to time standards, the standards should be changed if changes of methods are imposed.

Layman's methods The layman's methods (see Figure 7.12) do not require a lot of explanation except to distinguish between *estimating* and *analytical estimating*. The distinction can best be illustrated by a typical problem.

Activity

Consider the tasks listed below. Choose one that you know something about and estimate how long it should take one person to complete. Assume that the person doing the work is experienced and capable. (Five minutes.)

- Preparing a roast dinner for four people. The menu is roast lamb, roast potatoes, two vegetables.
- Completing a top overhaul on a Mini. This to include decoking the engine and regrinding the valves.
- Light cleaning of a classroom. This to include dusting all horizontal surfaces, wiping over all desks and chairs and sweeping the floor. Assume a classroom of 25 ft length and 16 ft width with desks for 20 students.

There is no 'correct answer' to this problem. We are asking you to think about the process of *how* you came to your 'standard time' value, rather than worry about the value itself. You will most probably have thought about the whole process and related your thinking to some previous occasion when you did a similar job. You will have considered the job as a whole. This is what we label as

- *estimating* – estimation based on previous experience, taking the job as a whole.

Suppose this method is not accurate enough? If we want to check it through in more detail we can write out each small part of the task and estimate for each part (or element) what we think the time should be. For example, for the roast dinner the elements might be:

	mins
Switch on oven, prepare meat	5
Measure out quantities of vegetables, prepare work area	5
Place meat in oven, commence preparation of vegetables	5
Peel potatoes	5
Prepare sprouts	10
Prepare carrots,	10
and so on	10

Activity

Take the task that you chose above and work through it in a similar way, estimating the time needed for each element. Find the total time. (Five minutes.)

You will see that the estimate lists the *sequence* of doing the work. In doing so, it gives a much more detailed statement of how the estimate was arrived at and therefore should give a more accurate estimate of the 'standard time' for the task. This process of breaking the task down into small parts in this way is

- *analytical estimating* – estimation based on previous experience but analysing the task element by element.

Time study   This is not a technique that you will use, but the work in your section may be subject to measurement by specialists; you should know the ideas that underpin time study, which is the most widely used method. In time study, the method is checked, agreed as satisfactory and then the time for a suitably skilled and experienced worker to do the work is measured.

If this time was taken as representative for all workers doing the work, it would be unsatisfactory, because workers vary in the speed that they work at, materials vary and conditions vary. Therefore a single time measurement on its own would not be satisfactory. To overcome this, the time is measured under *controlled conditions* which are carefully recorded on the time study sheet, and then corrected by calculation according to the *rating figure*. This is the judgement of the specialist who is taking the study, as to the degree of skill and effort applied by the worker.

There are three crucial parts of a time study (see Figure 7.13).

- A detailed description of the *elements of the task* being measured.
- *The time for each element*, measured by a stopwatch.
- The judgement, which is expressed as a number and is called the *rating*.

What to look out for: if you are supervisor of a section where a task is to be studied, there are a number of things that you have to be careful about.

Firstly you should make sure that the worker is as *near* average as possible, neither exceptionally fast nor slow, and is properly trained to do the job. Secondly make sure that the conditions are *typical for your department*. If the worker normally has to go and collect materials or tools from the other end of the department, make sure that this applies when the study is taken, and make sure that the specialist includes all these conditions in the study. Thirdly make sure that the specialist is *properly trained*. Finally, if the agreements in your organisation require

COMPONENT No.   *100983/A*   STUDY No.   *C/135*

COMPONENT NAME   *Transfer Switch*   TAKEN BY

OPERATION   *Assemble switch*   STUDY STARTED

OPERATOR   *J. Dickinson*   STUDY ENDED

DESCRIPTION	RATING	OBS. TIME	BASIC TIME	DESCRIPTION	RATING	OBS. TIME	BASIC TIME
① P.U. switch case	105	0·25		② P.U. switch cover	105	0·75	
w.l.h. place in jig	95	0·27		w.r.h. place onto	125	0·62	
P.U. switch core w.r.h.	115	0·23		switch case. P.U.4 off	105	0·73	
and place in switch	105	0·24		2BA screws assemble	95	0·80	
casing	100	0·25		to case w.r.h. Tighten with	95	0·75	
	100	0·25		air driver. Unclamp	100	0·75	
	80	0·30		and place completed	95	0·78	
	95	0·26		assy. aside at r.h.	105	0·72	

(Note that the observer has used some shorthand notation for speed. P.U. is 'pick up'; w.l.h. is 'with left hand'; w.r.h. is 'with right hand').

Fig 7.13   *Sample time study*

---

it, make sure that the appropriate *worker representatives* have been informed.

Rating: the judgement of the specialist is recorded as a number on a rating scale. The scale is labelled as the 0 to 100 rating scale, where the 100 point represents the standard performance for which we are trying to establish the time. Key points on this scale can be simply illustrated by written descriptions.

British Standard 0–100 rating scale	*Description*
50	Very slow, clumsy, fumbling, operator appears to have no interest.
75	Steady plod, deliberate, unhurried, time not being deliberately wasted.

100	Brisk, businesslike performance, as of a trained worker on piecework.
125	Very fast, operator shows a high degree of dexterity and skill.

A trained practitioner can judge a performance to within plus or minus 5 on this scale, and the entries in a time study will be on the intervals of 5 as in our example in Figure 7.13. This degree of accuracy in judgement is possible only for a trained observer who has regular practice sessions against known standards of performance.

Calculation of the standard time: for each observation the basic time is calculated thus:

basic time = observed time × (rating ÷ 100)

In Figure 7.13 the first entry was a rating of 105 and an observed time of 0.25 minutes, therefore:

basic time = 0.25 × (105 ÷ 100) = 0.2625

To simplify calculation, the times are usually rounded off to the nearest two figures after the decimal point, so the calculated figure entered in the basic time column of study will be 0.26.

After doing all the detailed calculations to arrive at the *Total Basic Time*, the time study practitioner will add on an allowance to cover actions which do not occur during the study, and an agreed amount of *relaxation time*. This is called the 'contingency and relaxation allowance' (CR allowance); it is usually between 10% and 20% depending on the nature of the work done. This gives us the standard time:

standard time = total basic time + CR allowance

for example

= (0.25 + 0.76) = 1.01 + 15% = 1.16 standard minutes

The standard time is the time that a trained worker would take to complete the task if he worked at a 100 performance and took all the allowances that had been incorporated in the study. This is how a time study is worked out; if you want to know more about the subject we recommended Dennis Whitmore's *Work Measurement* (Heinemann, 1987).

Uses of standard times: standard times can be used in many ways, most of which have some effect on the work of the supervisor. The more usual applications are:

- To plan the *schedule of work*.
- To assess *staff requirements* for a given workload.
- To plan the *most economic methods*.
- To calculate *direct labour costs*.
- To calculate *individual and departmental performance*.

The calculation of performance has the strongest impact on the supervisor because it is used by middle management as a *control*. 'I see that your index is down this week', they say. 'Why is that?' The calculation of performance is a reverse of the basic time calculation. The standard time is compared with the actual time taken, giving a performance figure which is similar to a rating:

performance = (standard time ÷ actual time taken) × 100

Suppose the standard time for cleaning a classroom is 0.85 standard hours and the person doing the work actually completes it in 0.75 hours. They have obviously worked faster than standard, and in fact their performance is in this case:

performance = (0.85 ÷ 0.75) × 100 = 113

Exercise 7.8

For the task above (0.85 standard hours.) calculate the performance achieved by workers doing exactly the same work who take 0.80 hours, 1.20 hours, 0.95 hours and 0.72 hours? (Five minutes.)

In exactly the same way departmental performances can be calculated for a period of work. If, say, for week 38 Tom Stranks's department produced 688 standard hours of work, and the clocked hours were 740 hours, then the departmental figure is:

departmental performance (week 38) : (688 ÷ 740) × 100 = 93

This is not quite up to standard, and Tom's manager may want to know why!

7.6 **Techniques to Help You Plan**

In Chapter 4, 'Getting the job done', we explained the factors involved in planning and the difficulties that can occur.

Self-check

How, in Chapter 4, did we define 'planning'? (Three minutes.)

Planning is thinking through the activities that have to be performed to complete the task and fitting them into a future time frame, taking account of the time that each activity takes and the logic of the process sequence.

We showed two plans on p. oo – a list-plan and a diagram-plan. In simple everyday sets of activities we carry the details in our heads. We do not write a plan or draw a diagram when we are about to do some gardening, or cook the dinner. But as things get more complicated or spread over a longer time scale, we have more need of records on paper, and we use diaries or calendars to keep an overview of all the activities. The technique called *Gantt charting* can help with more complex planning.

Gantt charts

Gantt charts are diagrams that incorporate the three main features of any plan – the time scale; the activities; and the resources used (see Figure 7.14).

Fig 7.14   *Gantt chart: essential features*

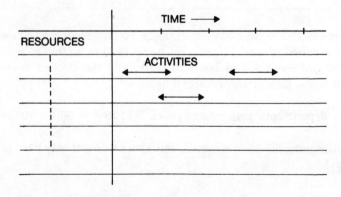

The resources and the activities will vary from one application to another. The *resources* might be machines, members of staff, classrooms; the *activities* might be production processes, work that operators are carrying out, different classes. The format is adaptable to all sorts of use and can be made up by drawing it out on paper or by purchasing one of the many proprietary systems that are on sale. The activities can be drawn or represented by self-adhesive labels or by magnetised rubber strip. Whatever the detail, the principle of the chart is the same: timescale on one side, resources on the other and activities fitted into the frame.

Using a Gantt chart If the staff in your section are allowed to take their holidays at any time between the end of March and the end of October, and you want to be certain that the section is capable of operating at all times, then you have to make sure that they are not all away at the same time. A Gantt chart can help to see the situation at a glance. Using squared paper, you can construct the chart like the one in Figure 7.15.

Activity

Look around at work and see how many examples of charts like this that you can find.

You will find holiday plans like our example, work schedules, machine records, training plans, vehicle bookings and many other applications of the Gantt chart.

Fig 7.15 *Sample Gantt chart: holiday arrangements*

STAFF	Mar.	Apr.	May	Jun.	Jul.	Aug.	Sept.	Oct.
Dicker, J.		▨				▨		
MacDonald, R			▨		▨			
Davies, J.						▨		
Mayor, R	▨							▨
Howard, C.				▨				
Gray, D.						▨		
Blume, J.					▨			
Thompson, G.							▨	▨

Working schedule by Gantt chart   In a small workshop there are five
machines, which we label A, B, C, D and E. The present workload
consists of four batches of work numbered I, II, III and IV. The
machines each perform different processes and the batches of work do
not go through the processes in the same sequence. We know the
required process sequence for each batch, and how long the process
takes for each machine. This information is tabulated below with the
process time in hours:

Batch I		Batch II		Batch III		Batch IV	
Machine	hours	Machine	hours	Machine	hours	Machine	hours
A	2	C	2	C	2	C	3
D	2	D	2	B	4	B	3
B	4	A	6	A	5	E	3
D	3	C	4	C	3	D	2
E	2	D	3				

This means that Batch III, for example, requires two hours on machine C
then four hours on B, followed by five hours on A and finally back to C
for another three hours to complete the batch.

To draw up a schedule to work these four batches through the
workshop in the least time, we can draw up the Gantt chart and enter the
activities. In preparing our version we have made certain assumptions.

- an eight hour working day;
- instant transfer to the next machine;
- a batch left overnight will not deteriorate;
- no process can start till the preceding process is completed.

First let us load Batch I. When we load Batch II we have to fit in around
the Batch I activities already entered and these impose delays on the
second batch (see Figure 7.16).

Exercise 7.9

Enter the Batch III and IV activities on the chart (Fig 7.16). How soon will all
four batches be completed? (Ten minutes.)

This gives us a complete picture of how the completion of the four
batches fits together when we load them in numerical order. But the
chart also now gives us a way of testing out other possibilities. Would the

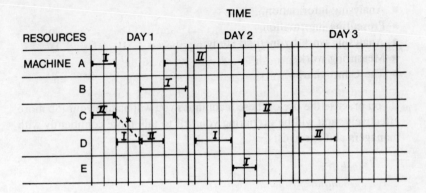

* Note delay imposed on Batch II because machine D is already on Batch I

Fig 7.16 *Gantt chart: work loading, batches I and II*

---

work be completed more quickly if we loaded Batch II in first? What would be the delay imposed if one of the operators was ill and there were only two available? Suppose we had to fit in a rush job which took precedence over the other batches?

Exercise 7.10

Redraw the Gantt chart blank from Figure 7.16 and enter the activities putting Batch II in first and fitting the other work in round it. Is this a quicker way to finish the four batches? (Fifteen minutes.)

These exercises show how useful the Gantt chart is for planning work where a number of activities have to be fitted in, and where scheduling and rescheduling are necessary as work loads change and new jobs are coming in all the time. It is a very useful tool for progressing the work as it proceeds.

7.7 Summary

This chapter has shown you some simple techniques which can help you perform more effectively as a supervisor:

- Analysing information.
- Presenting information.
- Analysing work by method study.
- Measuring work.
- The Gantt chart.

If you practise the use of these techniques you will handle your job more effectively, and will be preparing yourself to talk more confidently with managers and specialists.

8 Where Does the Supervisor Fit In?

In previous chapters we have concentrated on matters at the core of your job as a supervisor – what you do in the job, the skills that you need and the techniques that you might use to do the job better. However, the way that your daily work goes, and the difficulties that you meet in trying to do your job, will be largely determined by factors *outside the job*.

This chapter explains the more important of these influences. After you have worked through it, you will be able to analyse and handle them more confidently. They are subdivided into three parts: organisatonal factors; financial factors; and legal factors.

8.1 The Supervisor's 'Role'

Effects of size on the organisation

As organisations grow, other effects start to show which make the picture of the organisation more complicated. There may be more levels in the structure than previously, and so it will be necessary to take more care with *communications* to make sure that everybody works together properly. Another consequence of an increase in size is that the organisation comes to need, and can afford to employ, more specialists for particular parts of its work. Even small organisations have specialists, like the accountant who does the books. Large organisations have specialists in personnel management, industrial relations, quality control, work planning and others, according to the nature of their work. The company's organisation chart now comes to look something like that in Figure 8.1.

The boxes represent the *jobs* in the organisation; the solid lines show reporting lines along which the *authority is delegated*; and the dotted lines indicate the influence of the *specialists*.

Activity

Think about the organisation that employs you. Draw a similar diagram for your part of the organisation, showing the manager that you report to, your staff who you are responsible for, and the people at your level that you have regular contact with.

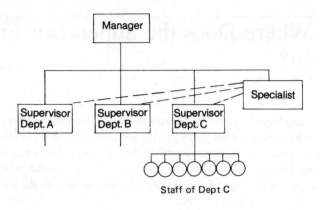

Fig 8.1   *Company organisation chart: levels in the structure*

To do this activity you have to think about the people that you have regular contact with. To make this more precise, in our analysis we refer to the position in the organisation as a 'role' – that is, any position which has a specified set of objectives, responsibilities and conditions of work. So for example, 'works manager' is a role, 'traffic controller' is a role, 'supervisor of X shop' is a role, 'management services officer' is a role, and so on. It is the *relationships between these roles* that are often not thought about carefully enough by the people who set up the organisation or change it around. As a person who occupies a role in an organisation you need to think carefully about the other roles that you relate to, and you need to separate in your mind the person from the role itself.

It may be that two people in your organisation do not get on well together in their work. Is it because their personalities are at odds, or is it their roles which cause the conflict?

Self-check

Consider a supervisor in charge of a production department. Identify three other roles in the organisation which might be in conflict with his because of the nature of their work. (Five minutes.)

There are a number of alternatives possible here, depending on the organisation that you have imagined. The most likely are:

- The *inspector* who is checking the work in the section and has to be sure that all the quality standards are met.
- The *production planners*, who will be imposing changes on work schedules to meet customer demands.
- The *management services staff*, who want to come into the department to study methods or set time standards.

This shows that supervisors in all organisations will be subject to the influence of specialist departments; if you are supervising a section you must be as clear as possible about the boundaries between your job and theirs.

Janet, Mark and Liz

Janet is the supervisor of the purchasing accounts section in a local company. She is responsible for making sure that the administrative work relating to the payment of accounts for items purchased by the company is carried out promptly, by running the section effectively and providing an administrative service to the purchasing department. The methods used in the section at the moment rely on some rather old machines for the calculation work, and electric typewriters to prepare the paperwork. The firm is in the process of changing over to computerised methods. The investigations as to the possible ways of doing this are being organised by Mark Thomas, who is a computer specialist seconded to Management Services to effect the changeover. A trial terminal has been installed in Janet's section to try out routines and help to overcome the fears that some of the staff have of such equipment. Last Tuesday, Mark Thomas came into the section to try out a new procedure. Janet was not in the section because she was at a business efficiency exhibition with her manager. Mark was under pressure from his boss to try out the idea, so he asked one of the girls, Liz, to drop the work that she was doing and to run his procedure on the terminal for that afternoon. Liz was not sure that this was right, but she felt that he was a senior man from another department and she had often seen him talking to Janet about the work; so she did what he asked. When Janet came back that afternoon and found that important routine work was not being done, she told Liz off. When Liz protested, Janet went to see Mark Thomas. The subsequent argument that arose soured the working relationship between Janet and Mark, and the installation was eventually delayed.

Exercise 8.1

Where did things go wrong? Draw a diagram representing the structure relating Janet, Mark and Janet's boss. (Ten minutes.)

This representation assumes that the roles were part of an organisational structure, which is normal for departments of this kind. It shows one of the most frequent forms of conflict between roles in organisations, which is the *overlap of the responsibilities* between the manager in the line (Janet) and the specialist (Mark). In some companies there are so many specialists that the supervisor is not sure whether he/she has a job left!

Formal and informal ways of getting things done

Short-cutting the formal procedure The story of Janet and Mark illustrates another feature of organisations. This is the presence side by side of a formal structure with formal (official) procedures, and informal (unofficial) ways of getting things done. As your diagram should indicate, there is a formal structure, but Mark's responsibility overlaps with Janet's. He has to get his development work done in a way which interferes with what Janet is trying to do, which is to keep the section running on routine output. So Mark resorted to informal methods. There are many supervisors who rely on getting things done by informal methods; they have their own contacts and can get things done quickly by having a 'word with Joe in the stores'; they operate on 'you scratch my back, I'll scratch yours'. Informal ways like this are a feature of all places of work; the more formal the organisation and the more rules that it has, the more likely it is that people will resort to informal methods, use short cuts and do deals with people who can help them.

Self-check

Is it justifiable to use informal methods to achieve results? (Five minutes.)

In certain circumstances you are justified in using informal methods to achieve results, but remember that they are only a 'bodge'. Some organisations are so overloaded with rules and regulations that to get anything done in a reasonable time needs informal short cuts of the formal procedure. The point is that informal methods are sometimes necessary but you should not come to rely on them as a regular way of working. As a short-term solution they are a possibility, but they are a symptom of some *fault in the organisation* – by continuing to use them you are not curing the fault. The ideal is to use them in the short term if necessary but also to do something to establish a way of working which is taken on by the organisation as the recognised way.

Talk to your manager You may have to refer some matter up to your manager for a solution. He is responsible for providing resources and support, just as you have a responsibility for your section. If you have a difficulty that hinders the work of your section, it might be an issue that he ought to take up with other managers at that level, or even higher. The most important working relationship for you is the one with your *immediate manager*. It should be a partnership in which each person is clear about what the other expects, and this will come about only if there are full exchanges of ideas and expectations. For you as a supervisor this is difficult if your manager does not communicate much, but you can start the process off. The key to this is your *statement of objectives*. If you have written down your objectives and key areas of responsibility as we explained in Chapter 4, show them to your manager and ask him if he agrees. This will clarify your expectations of each other, but it may not be easy and you will have to stick at it. The aim is to get everybody pulling in the same direction.

8.2 **Supervisors and the Financial System**

Another aspect of the surrounding organisation that affects supervisors is the financial system. This is the field of another set of specialists – the accountants. It is not our intention to go into any depth on financial matters, or turn you into a specialist, but supervisors do need to know in outline how the money system works. This section aims to provide that outline.

Accountants control the financial inflows and outflows as well as the control of internal costs. This is where the supervisor has a part to play because, as someone in charge of a working group, you are a vital point where costs are incurred. Remember, *every action generates a cost*.

Fixed and variable costs

From Chapter 4, you will remember that we examined the problems of a sports club who were planning a dance. Now let us look at this from a financial point of view. They have found from their search for information that the fixed costs will be:

Hire of the hall	£40
Band	90
Print costs	30

They have decided to provide a meal during the evening, and estimate that if they do it with volunteers the cost for each meal will be £2, which will be added into the price of the ticket. They then have to make a decision: how much to charge for each ticket?

Self-check

What is the other factor which they will have to consider before they can decide on the price of a ticket? (Two minutes.)

Apart from the costs already listed, there will be one other main factor which will influence their decision – the numbers that they expect to come to the dance. This is not easy to judge because it is one of those double-sided decisions, in that the price of the ticket will affect the number of people who will come, and this in turn will affect the price that they can charge for each ticket. How will they decide? They will consider the costs and see that some of the costs are fixed irrespective of how many people come, such as the hire of the hall and the cost of the band. However, the cost of the food will vary according to the number of people who buy tickets.

Suppose they make a stab at the ticket price and decide to charge £5 per ticket. On each ticket there will be a cost of £2 for the meal and this will leave £3 to help towards the fixed costs.

Self-check

On this basis, how many tickets will they have to sell to cover their fixed costs? (Five minutes.)

The fixed costs have been given as: band £90, hall £40 and printing £30, a total fixed cost of £160. If each ticket sold contributes £3 to covering fixed costs, they will have to sell 160 ÷ 3 = 53.3 or, to be more realistic 54 tickets to exceed fixed costs slightly. What is more exciting is that every ticket that they sell after the 54th will contribute £3 to club funds, as a sort of profit. We can represent this on a diagram if we draw a scale up the side marked off to measure the costs, and a scale along the bottom to indicate the numbers of tickets sold. On this we draw a line showing

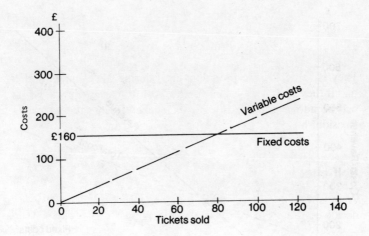

Fig 8.2 *Graph of fixed and variable costs*

the cost of meals, which increases as a number of people increases (variable costs), and another line which stays the same however many people come (fixed costs) (see Figure 8.2).

To make Figure 8.2 more useful, we want it to show *total costs*, which are fixed plus variable costs, and we draw variable costs on top of fixed to represent this. Also, we add another line to Figure 8.2 to show the money coming from the ticket sales (called *revenue*) (see Figure 8.3).

Self-check

What is the significance of the point in Figure 8.3 where the revenue line crosses the total cost line? (Two minutes.)

The break-even point
The point where the two lines cross is where revenue just equals the total costs, or, in other words, where the club has just covered its costs but is making no profit. It is *breaking even,* and the point at which this happens is called the *break-even point*. Figure 8.3 makes up a model of the situation and shows the organisers just what profit they can make at different sales levels. We know from the previous calculation that the break-even number is 54 and that every ticket sold after that adds £3 to club funds. This is shown by the growing gap between the revenue line and the total cost line.

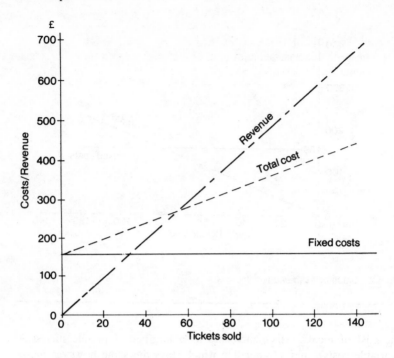

Fig 8.3   *Graph of revenue and total costs*

Exercise 8.2

From Figure 8.3, find out what the profit would be if they sold 140 tickets. check your figure by a calculation. (Ten minutes.)

They make a good profit, but it does depend on selling those 140 tickets. They could consider increasing the price of each ticket in order to make more profit (this would be shown by a steeper revenue line in Figure 8.3), but in doing so they will make it harder to sell tickets.

The cost per unit
Another important feature of costs is shown if we work out the cost for each person as the numbers increase. If the dance was a disaster and they sold only one ticket, the total cost for that ticket would be £160 fixed costs plus £2 for the food cost. Not a very likely situation, but the cost of running the dance for that one person would be £162! If they sold two

tickets, the fixed cost per ticket would be 160 ÷ 2 = £80, plus the £2 variable cost per person, giving a total cost per person of £82. To examine how this cost per unit (the ticket sold in this case) changes as sales increase, we can draw up a simple table:

No. of tickets sold	1	2	3	5	10	30	50	100	200
Fixed cost	160	160	160	160	160	160	160	160	160
Variable cost	2	4	6	10	20	60	100	200	400
Total cost	162	164	166	170	180	220	260	360	560
Cost per unit	162	82	55	34	18	7.3	5.2	3.6	2.8

Exercise 8.3

What is the unit cost per ticket if they sell, 70, 110, 150? (Five minutes.)

Notice that the variable cost per ticket stays the same, but amount of the fixed cost that each ticket carries *declines rapidly as they sell more*. This effect can be shown by drawing the unit cost line on the same axes as we drew the cost lines, as in Figure 8.4.

Fig 8.4 *Graph of cost per unit figures*

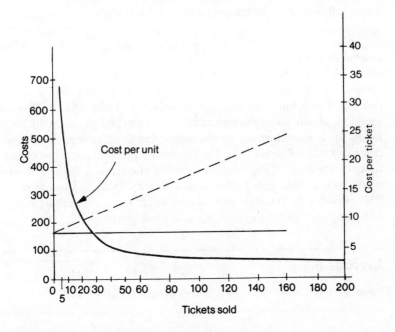

This idea of reduction in unit cost is of vital importance to you as a supervisor, because in your section there are some fixed and some variable costs, and the *more work you get out of the section* the *lower the cost per unit* will become. The basic unit will vary from one section to another. In manufacturing it will be the units or items that are being produced, in catering the cost per meal, in printing the cost per book, in transport the cost per mile. Somewhere there will be a *unit of measurement* to relate the costs to.

Covering the fixed costs

The problem of earning enough money on each job to pay the fixed costs is a preoccupation for the cost accountant. He or she has the job of looking after the *internal costs* of the business. In most cases the situation is rather more complicated than selling tickets, because there will be a mix of work going through the business. A range of products or services is offered by most businesses, and the cost accountant has to make sure that each job is charged to the customer at such a rate that costs are covered. Fixed costs are called overheads. Expenses such as rent and rates, insurances, audit fees and the salaries of staff who do not make a direct contribution to the product fall into this category. Any cost which cannot be charged to a specific unit of outputs is an overhead, and has to be paid for. To recover money to pay for the overheads, the accountant will calculate the variable costs in any new job (such as material and labour costs) and then add on a percentage to call in money on that job which will contribute to the payment of indirect costs.

Control of costs

Where does all the money go? In a business, the control of costs is complicated by the fact that it is not just one project that they are concerned with but a whole range of activities. There will be different products, all streaming through at different rates and all due at different times. To cope with this, the accountant has to make sure that *proper control of internal costs* exists. The accountant prepares a forecast of cash flow, on the basis of information from the managers of the operational work, such as anticipated sales, required stock levels and labour costs. This provides the *financial plan* against which *actual expenditure* can be compared thus giving the start of the control system.

Exercise 8.4

What are the five elements of a control system? (Five minutes.)

Let us now work through an example which shows how the financial plan is used as the basis for control of costs and expenditure.

Hughes Furniture

Mike Gibbs

Mike Gibbs supervises a small unit which makes traditional wooden chairs which sell to retailers for £45 each. The unit consists of Mike himself as foreman and three members of staff, a woodworking machinist, an assembler and a finisher. Mike runs the unit and is accountable to the owner, Mr Hughes. Mike is laying out the financial plan for the next six months to submit to Mr Hughes, and there are these facts which have to be taken into account:

- fixed costs for premises and equipment are £1,900 per month;
- wages are £160 per week for each of the three operators;
- Mike's salary is £800 per month;
- material costs are £20 per chair and material is purchased and paid for in the month that it is needed.
- Mike has worked out with Mr Hughes the anticipated demand for the next six months, as shown below:

Jan.	Feb.	Mar.	Apr.	May	Jun.
150	210	250	300	300	280

Mike lays out the plan in a table taking each entry in turn. The cost figures are easy to lay out since the fixed costs are regular each month, and wages can be calculated as a monthly expenditure.

	£
Three operators at £160 per week each:	
3 × 160 = 480 per week × 4 = monthly wages	1920
Foreman's monthly salary:	800
Total labour cost per month:	2720

Material costs are calculated at £20 for each chair.

Exercise 8.5

What will be the material costs for each month as planned? (Two minutes.)

We can now assemble all these facts into a table of costs. For each month we enter into the table the items of cost expenditure. For example, for January, we know fixed costs are £1,900, wages £1920, salaries £800 and materials £3000 giving a total expenditure of £7120.

Calculation of revenue

Expenditure is one side of the equation and we need to know the other, which is the revenue that will be earned from sales. In Mike's business there is no stock holding, as chairs are made only to order, but there is one month's credit, which means that the money for chairs made in January will not be received until February. The outstanding revenue from December's sales is £10,000.

Exercise 8.6

What will the revenue be for the other five months? (Five minutes.)

We can now enter these figures with the costs, and calculate the profit or loss that the unit will earn in each month if the forecast comes true, and if costs can be held to their estimated values.

	Jan	*Feb*	*Mar*	*Apr*	*May*	*Jun*
Forecast	150	210	250	300	300	280
Fixed costs	1 900	1 900	1 900	1 900	1 900	1 900
Wages	1 920	1 920	1 920	1 920	1 920	1 920
Salaries	800	800	800	800	800	800
Materials	3 000	4 200	5 000	6 000	6 000	5 600
Total expenditure	7 620	8 820	9 620	10 620	10 620	10 220
Revenue	10 000	6 750	9 450	11 250	13 500	13 500
Balance	+ 2380	− 2070	− 170	+ 630	+ 2880	+ 3280

How do we use the forecast?

A table of financial information like this is important to the firm for several reasons. Firstly, it is a *plan* and shows if the business will succeed in the coming period or whether it will be overdrawn at the bank. In this particular example the business is not doing terribly well, since if we add up the plus and minus balances on the bottom line, the business will make in this six months £6930, which means it is just ticking over and not making much profit. They would have to decide what to do about that, whether to sell more actively to get more orders and generate more revenue, or to cut costs in some way.

Secondly, the table provides a way of telling what the *cash needs* of the business are. As the plan stands, the maximum amount overdrawn will be £2070, in February. If they received a big order which was not paid until the order was complete, then that would affect cash flow and require further overdrafts. This would be all right if the bank was prepared to extend the overdraft, but if not the business would collapse. Many firms have gone out of business in just this way.

Thirdly, the forecast now provides a series of monthly statements of *expected expenditure and income* (costs and revenue) which is spent and as money comes in, the supervisor can monitor this against the plan and try to take corrective action. If costs increase above the planned levels, or if material prices change, or if there is any interruption to production which will consequently affect revenue, then the effects can be predicted and action taken. The statement for each month becomes the budget for that period and provides the standard for budgetary control. In real life where things are more complicated than in our example, each part of the operation has its own budget – there will be a sales budget, a production budget, and so on.

The supervisor's role in the financial system

In all companies, supervisors have a part to play in the business. You are in control of the working group that helps to *earn revenue but generates cost*. The section must earn its keep even if it is not costed and budgeted in a detailed way. In this brief look at the financial surroundings, we have shown five important ideas.

Self-check

What are the five ideas that you should remember about costs and revenue in the business? (Ten minutes.)

- The way in which the work of the organisation generates *cash revenues*. Cash will flow into the firm only if products and services, which provides customer satisfaction, flow out of it.
- Some costs are *fixed* in relation to the volume of work; others *vary*.
- *Total costs* must be matched against *revenue* to see whether you are making a profit or a loss.
- The importance of keeping volume of work up to spread the fixed costs and thus keep the *cost per unit down*.
- The value of *forecasting revenue and costs* as a basis for calculating cash needs, and using budgetary control to keep costs down.

8.3 **Legal Factors**

In this section we look at supervisors and their position in common law. We establish their position in law and then examine the legal implications of some Acts of Parliament that confer rights on employees. We refer to your staff as 'employees' in this section to conform with the wording of parliamentary statutes, codes of practice, etc.

Supervisors need to know about the *rights of their employees* in order to manage them effectively. We look at Acts that are of specific interest to supervisors, followed by an introduction to the Health and Safety at Work Act 1974 (and its 1987 amendment). Finally, we look at the role of trade unions and how they affect the supervisor.

Common law

Every employer has a *duty of care* towards his employees. The supervisor, as the employer's representative, has the same duty. Supervisors, by the very nature of their jobs, are also *representatives of the employees*, who have a right to expect their supervisor to represent them to management. Because supervisors are the first line managers they are often in a better position to exercise this duty of care than senior managers. Supervisors have a legal duty to represent management on the one side and their employees on the other, which makes their jobs very difficult when the two sides are in dispute. By virtue of their position in the organisation supervisors have a *legal right to give orders*, provided the orders are legal and reasonable. They must expect that all reasonable orders will be executed otherwise they could not carry out their jobs. We make this point because this is the fundamental authority that supervisors have, although the right to give an order may become the focus of a dispute.

Discipline

Supervisors are responsible to management for the *actions of their employees*. One of the duties of supervisors is maintaining discipline.

Activity

Has your company got a disciplinary procedure? Are you familiar with it? (Five minutes.)

You should be aware of the steps in your company's disciplinary procedure, and exactly what your *role and function is within it*. Does your company's disciplinary procedure conform to the code of practice laid down by the Advisory, Conciliation and Arbitration Service (ACAS) who have a duty to improve industrial relations. If it does not, you could be at a legal disadvantage. Any case referred to ACAS or an industrial tribunal will automatically be judged against this code of practice. If your company does not have a procedure, or if its procedure does not conform to the code, you should get a copy for your reference.

These are the essential features of disciplinary procedures as recommended by ACAS. Disciplinary procedures should not be viewed primarily as a means of *imposing sanctions against the individual concerned*. They should be designated to emphasise and encourage improvement in conduct. (See Chapter 6, where we explain disciplinary interviews.) Disciplinary procedures should:

- Be *in writing*.
- Specify *to whom they apply*.
- Provide for matters to be dealt with *quickly*.
- Indicate the *disciplinary actions* which may be taken.
- Specify the levels of management which have the *authority to take the various forms of disciplinary actions*, ensuring that immediate superiors do not normally have the power to dismiss without reference to senior management.
- Provide for individuals to be *informed* of the complaints against them and to be given an opportunity to *state their case* before decisions are reached.
- Give individuals the right to be *accompanied by a trade union representative* or by a *fellow employee of their choice*.
- Ensure that, except for gross misconduct, no employees are dismissed for a *first breach of discipline*.
- Ensure that disciplinary action is not taken until the case has been carefully *investigated*.
- Ensure that individuals are given an *explanation* for any penalty imposed.
- Provide a *right of appeal* and specify the procedure to be followed.

Grievance

No matter how careful we are, sometimes individuals feel they have a grievance. A good supervisor will always 'sort out' a grievance as soon and as smoothly as possible. To do this one needs common sense, knowledge of grievance procedures, knowledge of the job, and other company data.

Most organisations have both *informal* as well as *formal* procedures; often the informal precede the formal. Always go for an informal solution as less red tape is involved, fewer people ('outsiders') get involved and there is seldom a written record kept! This last point may be the very reason to go for the formal procedure – when the objective is to amass evidence to be used later!

Typical informal procedure   The steps in the procedure are:

- An attempted resolution by *direct approach* between the parties concerned.
- If this does not work out an *interview* is requested at a senior level. Within a stipulated time (laid down in the procedure) a *meeting* is held with both parties, their respective 'friends', and the senior member of the organisation.
- If this fails, the procedure usually allows for a *repeat performance* at a higher level.

Typical formal procedure   Should the informal procedure fail to provide a solution the formal procedure may be undertaken.

Here, the steps are:

- *Written notice of the grievance* is sent to a nominated officer (designated in the organisation's formal procedure) with copies to the second party.
- Within a stipulated time a *meeting* is convened to hear *evidence* from parties concerned. The powers that are brought to bear on attendance vary with the organisation and the seriousness of the grievance. Friends are usually in attendance.
- There is invariably an *appeals procedure* to cover the eventuality that the formal procedure does not procure a satisfactory solution.

8.4 **The Employment Protection Act 1978**

This Act brought together four earlier Acts which covered the rights of the individual employee:

- Redundancy Payments Act 1965
- Contracts of Employment Act 1972
- Trade Union and Labour Relations Act 1974
- Employment Protection Act 1975

The 1978 Act has been substantially updated and amended since it was first passed; the four important additions that will concern you are:

- Employment Act 1980
- Employment Act 1982
- Employment Act 1988
- Trade Union Act 1984

You should make sure that as a supervisor you have read the parts of the employment legislation relevant to your own work area; we shall now discuss the most important topics in brief detail

The rights of employees
Under the provisions of the Act, employees' rights are set out under the following eight headings; employees are entitled to a written statement of their contract of employment with these details included.

Contracts of employment

- First – after four weeks the employee is given the right to a specified *period of notice*.
- Second – within thirteen weeks the employer must provide the employee with a written statement of their contract giving all *necessary details of employment*.
- Third – the Act contains rules for computing *continuity of employment* (for pension-related matters).

Itemised pay statements   Itemised pay statements must be provided for all employees, showing *gross pay*, *take-home pay* and *details of all deductions*.

Guaranteed pay   Employees are guaranteed entitlement to receive payments for up to five days a quarter, at a rate which is reviewed annually, in compensation for *loss of earning due to circumstances in the employer's control*.

Time off work   Employees who are *trade union officials* are entitled to time off for trade union duties, or training with pay if the union is recognised by the employer. Trade union members are entitled to time off for union meetings. *Pregnant women* are entitled to time off for prenatal care. Under certain circumstances, employers are required to permit employees who hold *specified public positions* reasonable time off to perform duties associated with them. Workers being made redundant are also entitled to time off to *look for work*.

Rights of expectant mothers   The rights of the expectant mother are detailed in the Social Services Act 1986. She cannot be dismissed because of pregnancy. She is entitled to get her job back up to twenty-nine weeks after the baby's birth, or a suitable alternative job and statutory maternity pay, after two years' continuous service. After 6 months service she is entitled only to statutory maternity pay.

Unfair dismissal   Employees who have satisfied certain minimum periods (104 weeks) of employment have a right not to be unfairly dismissed and have access to machinery in case of complaint through *industrial tribunals*. Remedies for unfair dismissal are stated as reinstatement, re-engagement or compensation. Written statements for reason for dismissal are a right for employees with more than *104 weeks* employment.

A particular area of interest to the supervisor is that of 'constructive dismissal'. This arises when an employee leaves employment and claims that this was *as a result of their treatment*. This employee would claim that he was constructively dismissed.

Fair dismissal   Dismissal can be fair only if the employer can show that the reason for it was one of those listed below:

- a reason related to the employee's *capability* or *qualifications* for the job;
- a reason related to the employee's *conduct*;
- *redundancy*;
- a *statutory duty or restriction* which prevents the employment being continued;
- some other *substantial reason* which could justify the dismissal.

The employer must also show that he or she acted *reasonably* in the circumstances in treating that reason as sufficient to justify dismissing the employee.

Redundancy   In the case of redundancy an employee is compensated with a lump sum called a 'redundancy payment' related to length of continuous service, age and pay when statutory conditions are met. The employee is entitled to a *statement of the sums to be paid* prior to payment.

8.5 **Other Acts that Affect the Supervisor**

- Equal Pay Act 1970
- Rehabilitation of Offenders Act 1974
- Sex Discrimination Act 1975 and 1986
- Race Relations Act 1976

As a supervisor you may be responsible for selecting employees for training and promotion, and for appointing new employees. Most of these tasks are carried out through interviews, and all the four Acts, quite rightly, make it unlawful to discriminate against an individual. 'Discrimination' means treating any person *less favourably than others* because of specific grounds.

Equal Pay Act 1970
You must treat, pay and provide equal prospects to men and women employed on 'like work' – in other words, not discriminate. In the event of complaint under this Act, an employee may appeal to an *industrial tribunal*.

Rehabilitation of Offenders Act 1974
You must not discriminate against persons who have a *criminal record*, and you must take reasonable steps to ensure that others do not discriminate against them during their period of rehabilitation, which varies with their sentence.

Sex Discrimination Act 1975 and 1986
This Act protects against discrimination against anyone on grounds of *sex* or *marital status*; its provisions include victimisation because a person has previously complained under this Act. Appeals are dealt with by the Equal Opportunities Commission.

Race Relations Act 1976
This protects against discrimination on grounds of *colour*, *race*, *nationality*, *ethnic*, or *national origins*.

Direct and indirect discrimination

Direct discrimination   Direct discrimination occurs when discrimination is *solely because* of colour, race or origin.

Indirect discrimination   Indirect discrimination occurs when conditions adversely affect a *particular group more than others*; for example, using a complicated language test for selection purposes. Job applicants, or existing employees, wishing to make a case case use the conciliation service of ACAS or the Commission for Racial Equality.

Self-check

How should you distinguish between direct and indirect discrimination at work? (Two minutes.)

Direct discrimination takes place when it is directly applied on grounds of colour, race, creed, sex or marital status. Indirect discrimination takes place when conditions adversely affect the individual or group through the medium of language, knowledge or any other requirement or condition, whether intentional or not. These two types of discrimination apply to all four Acts.

Health and Safety at Work, etc. Act 1974 (and amendments 1987)
This Act supplanted the cumbersome Factories Acts, and carries the main thrust of a continuing campaign to ensure safe, healthy working conditions for employees. The Act provides for the gradual replacement of health and safety requirements by revising and updating provisions, in the form of a system of *regulations* and *approved codes of practice* prepared in consultation with industry to create an integrated body of requirements enforced on a common basis.

Whatever your employment, you will find a code of practice covering your appropriate needs. These codes have *legal status* and, while they are not statutory, will be used in legal proceedings as evidence that statutory requirements have been contravened.

This is similar in practice to the Highway Code (of Practice). If you have an accident, and are found not to be sticking to the code then that would be evidence of failure in your duty of care.

Activity

Get a copy of any of the codes of practice relating to your place of work, and read it carefully.

Duties   As explained earlier, you represent the employer who has certain specific duties under the 1974 Act. For example, all plant and equipment must be kept up to the necessary *safety standards*. All *systems* *of work* must be safe; this includes the environment in which you work. You are responsible for the regular inspection of all safety equipment, which includes safety access arrangements, testing devices and protective and extraction equipment. The safe storage of harmful 'substances' is another duty (see COSHH, below).

Policy organisation and arrangements The employer is responsible for providing a *written statement* of general safety policy, showing the organisation and arrangements for health and safety at work.

Safety information and training Safety information and training are the duty of every employer. If there are processes on your section that may require special training needs it is up to you to ensure that they are *identified* and that *adequate training* is provided to ensure the safety of your staff.

What does this all mean? You, as the employer's representative, must make sure that your workplace is safe. You have the full power of the law to back you. You must stop any unsafe practices and also report them to your health and safety representative and to your manager. You must also stop any unsafe, unhealthy conditions that you see or that are brought to your attention.

As the supervisor, you may be liable in negligence of supervision if one of your employees has negligently caused damage to another person. People who are injured usually want compensation and their first step is to *prove negligence*. As the employer has the money, he is normally sued. As his representative, you could be in the firing line. You could also be liable under the Occupier's Liability Act 1957, whereby all occupiers owe a duty of care to all persons *lawfully on their premises*. You would be the 'occupier' in the boss's absence.

Employees They, too, have a duty to take reasonable care to avoid injury to themselves or others by their work activities. Your work instructions should point out any hazards in execution to operators or workmates.

Interference with, or misuse of, any item provided for health, safety and welfare is a *criminal offence*, punishable by fine and/or imprisonment. Individuals may be prosecuted in a civil court for negligence if they cause damage to another individual.

Activity

What action should you take against an employee you see tampering with a safety sign? (Five minutes.)

As a supervisor you would use the normal disciplinary procedures on seeing the employee tampering with the safety sign. In addition, under the Act you have provision for reporting this incident to the Health and Safety Executive, with fine or imprisonment as possible consequences.

COSHH The Control of Substances Hazardous to the Health (COSHH) Act becomes law on 1 October 1989, and will control a range of substances which it is felt could be harmful to our health.

8.6 The Supervisor and Trade Unions

You may belong to a trade union. Being a supervisor does not prevent you joining a union. There are unions specially organised for supervisors – e.g. the Association of Scientific, Technical and Managerial Staffs (ASTMS). The organisation for which you work has a hierarchy designed specifically for the production of goods, or the supply of service, by their employees. Trade unions also have a hierarchy that descends from national level, through regional, district, and branch level, down to shop stewards who represent the same employees. You as a supervisor represent management, at the first level, to these employees.

Supervisors come into conflict with unions, as a result of disputes with employees who are union members. If your firm recognises the union and has entered into joint consultation with them then you could easily find yourself in the position where your employees, who are union representatives, are negotiating with and have access to information not available to you. Any of your employees who are trade union members are entitled to attend union meetings. Trade union representatives are entitled to time off with pay for union duties.

Supervisors should be careful that all treatment of union representatives is fair, or it may be seen as 'victimisation'. There are special notes for treatment of union officials laid down in the ACAS code of practice.

Management means getting things done through people, while trade unions are about getting things for people. These two ideologies can exist in harmony. You as a supervisor, right in the middle of the game, can play a large part in ensuring that harmony is promoted. You are close to the workforce and can sort out problems as soon as they appear. Good industrial relations are good sense, and will make your job easier to handle and your employer's business more efficient.

We have looked at the legal implications of your supervisory role, and perhaps given you an idea of this important aspect of your job. If you want more information on any of these topics try your employer, union, jobcentre and library, in that order.

To find out more about this vital subject also please read:

Chris Brewster, *Employee Relations,* and Margaret Attwood, *Personnel Management*, both in the Macmillan Professional Masters Series.

9 Pulling it All Together

Being a supervisor is a tough job, but a crucial one. it is all too often undervalued by employers. Very often people are promoted to the job of supervisor because of technical competence, or because they have been in the job for a long time. In most cases, supervisors are expected to know how to supervise but are not given the training which would help them do this effectively. The job of the supervisor is difficult, and needs proper training. If you have not had training as a supervisor, you should examine the possibilities of attending a course of study in supervisory management at a local college of further education.

The examining authority for the subject is the National Examination Board for Supervisory Management (NEBSM); the qualification obtained is the Certificate in Supervisory Management, which is recognised by many employers as necessary for promotion to the position of supervisor, and entitles the holder to membership of the Institute of Supervisory Management. Apart from the certificate in supervisory management, NEBSM also runs introductory and diploma courses.

Recognition of supervisors as an important level of management will come about only when supervisors *see themselves as a profession* – that is, as a group of trained professional people with their own representative body, recognised by employers as speaking for all supervisors. This function is carried out by the Institute of Supervisory Management (ISM) at 22 Bore Street, Lichfield, Staffs, WS13 6LP. You should write to them and see what they can offer you.

We make no pretence about the demands of supervision. We know that you will have difficulty finding solutions to the problems you meet. Do not expect instant success. Take your time and make gradual progress. Remember, in reading this book that you have acquired *knowledge*; the skills needed to put this knowledge *into effect* require practice.

You have to translate our ideas into a working arrangement which suits you and your team. Only you can do this, with thought, care and, above all, sensitivity. Think and look before you leap.

In writing this book we have had to separate the elements of supervision to make them easier to explain. Real life does not come at you in separated, packaged problems; it comes as a mixed, and sometimes confusing, stream of activity. All the sections of this book fit together in your job and might crop up at any time in your working day.

When things are running smoothly, you will have a responsible job; when problems occur, you will really show your worth. You will be at the centre of things; other people will be involved; you will have to communicate effectively; and solutions will have to be found. Do not be afraid to ask for help if you need it, once you have evaluated the situation.

Self-check

Go back to the case of Tom Stranks in Chapter 1 and read it again. List the various implications of the incident. How could Tom use this book to help him? (Ten minutes.)

There is a lot going on in this incident. Here are some points you should have listed:

- Tom is *misusing his time* rectifying parts from other departments, instead of supervising his staff.
- There were *no records* of this rectification.
- Tom *missed the meeting*.
- His manager is under pressure and is copying by switching supervisors around. Both he and Tom are *'fire-fighting'*. Are there legal implications in putting Tom on to Tony's section?
- Tom needs to be clear just what his *objectives* are. This will give him the confidence to spell out to Bill Betts just what the consequences of his decisions are likely to be.
- Tom is being used to tell Tony, and he will have to use all his *social skills* to avoid conflict with Tony on D line.
- The effect of Bill's instructions on the staff of both A and D lines will be to create *uncertainty* which will have a bad effect on their morale and their work.
- There are indications that *planning* in the company is poor. There is a lot of *ad hoc* decision making, and the control systems seem to be inadequate.

There is plenty of information for Tom and his problems in this book:

- Tom would benefit from identifying his *supervisory tasks* and concentrating on them (Chapter 2).
- By rectifying the faulty components, Tom is depriving the company of valuable *control information* and appearing to be less productive (Chapter 5).

- Missing the meeting might indicate that Tom does not *plan or organise effectively* (Chapters 4 and 7).
- Bill is not dealing with Tony – the real problem. He is using Tom to do his dirty work in an unorthodox way. Tom is in an awkward position if Tony *refuses to accept his authority* in Bill's absence (Chapter 8).
- *Tom's objectives* are unclear (Chapter 4).
- Tony could represent a human relations problems for Tom which might be overcome if Tom could handle people and know how to deal with *conflict* (Chapter 3).
- The effects on A and D line staff could be minimised by *sensitive briefing*, *skilful leadership* and *positive motivation* (Chapters 3, 5 and 6).
- If Tom had his *own section* well planned, organised and controlled, perhaps he would be in a better position to convince Bill that the company needed some help in these and other areas.

You can see that in one small incident, many of the topics covered in this book have come together. Every day at work the same sort of incident could – and does – happen to you. The threads that run through the separate sections of the book are woven together to make up the whole supervisory picture.

9.1 How Can I be Expected to Cope?

Being a supervisor means you have to cope with the 'threads' of real-life situations. You have to be good at getting the best results from people, quick to react when things go wrong, and able to maintain control. The job often means that you have to work under pressure and be capable of coping with the stress that it brings.

The essential aspects of working under pressure seem to be the same for all jobs, and you will have developed your own ways of doing this. Pressure arises when you have too much to do in too little time, or inputs arrive too rapidly to cope with them. If you do not do something to relieve the pressure, you make mistakes, increasing the pressure and stress. It is the way that you *perceive things* that creates stress: it is all in the mind. What some people see as threatening is seen by others as a challenge, an opportunity to be creative, a chance to act.

Pressure
To reduce the pressure on you, be prepared to put limits on the work that you are willing to take on. This may mean saying to your manager, 'You can have either this *or* that'. It is better to concentrate on a limited range

of things, and do them well, than to take on everything that people ask of you and leave a trail of half-finished jobs behind. If you plan ahead, anticipating possible difficulties, having alternative plans and some slack available to cope with emergencies, you will reduce the stress of crisis management. If your work is such that there are many crises and interruptions, you must allow more slack between tasks. If you are planning or organising projects for months ahead, and cannot fit them into your normal working day, earmark a period a week or two ahead specifically for these long-term tasks. Get your staff, and your manager, to protect you from interruption during that time so that you get on with the project.

You can reduce pressure by doing the following:

Long term

- Get your *objectives* clear.
- *Plan ahead*; anticipate difficulties.
- Know your *limits*.
- Be prepared to *limit your inputs*.

Every day

- Establish *priorities* – review them frequently.
- *Do one job at a time*; concentrate on it, and finish it.
- Give time to *planning* even under pressure.
- *Involve your staff*. They like to feel wanted.
- *Tidy as you go*; keep your workplace tidy – it is a reflection of the sort of person you are.
- Evaluate the consequences of *putting off* or *not taking* action.
- Be prepared to *adjust the quality of your work*. It is better to deliver an adequate job on time than a perfect job too late.

Activity

Read the last section of Chapter 4 again, 'Organising your daily work'. Have you written down a clear statement of your job objectives and key areas of responsibility?

If not, *do it now*. This statement is a cornerstone of many of the activities of a supervisor or manager. Organising your time, delegating, coping with pressure, all require this clear understanding of the job. Look at Ian's example in Chapter 4 if you are not sure how to write it.

If the going seems hard, do not moan and complain – see what you can do to *improve it*. You will meet plenty of people who are always complaining, always blaming others, saying 'it's not my fault'. They do this to relieve their own frustrations, and it serves a purpose *for them*, but it does not get anything done. If you find yourself complaining, if things are getting you down, try to think positively about the issue. Ask, 'What can we do about it?' There is nearly always a solution; get on and do something about it. If there appears to be no solution, then you may have to put up with the situation. There is one other possibility: maybe *you* are the problem.

Do not assume that you cannot do things. Be prepared to test the limits of your freedom of action. Lots of people seem to erect limits which they feel are as far as they can got. They say:

- 'We could not do that because the gaffer would not approve'; or
- 'It's against company policy'; or
- 'You will never get Planning to agree to that'.

If you think this way, you restrict your action inside the real limits of your potential. Test how far you can go without being extreme and you will find that the real limits of freedom lie *beyond those that you think exist*. The good manager says, 'Do whatever you think necessary to get the job done. I'll tell you whether you are going too far or not far enough.' You have got to find out where the limits are. If in doubt, ask yourself this question: 'What would a good, confident supervisor do in this situation?'

9.2 Look After Staff

The best results from your section will be achieved only if you obtain the best from the people who work under your supervision. You have to treat them as *people* rather than *resources*. They are individuals with their own qualities, and their own worries and problems, which will affect their attitudes and their approach to work.

Activity

In the interests of efficiency and better organisation you have decided to change the present work groupings on your section. How might they see this action as a threat? (Ten minutes.)

People become set in their ways and are resistant to change. They see change as threatening:

- their *security* and *skills*;
- their *status* and *position*;
- the *respect* of their mates;
- their *promotion* and *development*;
- their *links with friends* in existing groups.

To 'sell' change, you will have to reassure the people concerned honestly that their fears are groundless.

The way your staff respond to situations such as we have outlined will depend on their *attitudes towards you*. If you have earned their respect and trust, your chances of effecting change will be much higher. It is your job to ensure that they have the resources to do the work, and this may mean that you have to negotiate with management on behalf of your section, and press for the conditions that you and your team need.

Give encouragement

Another important aspect of achieving good results is to give encouragement. You should try to set up a *positive cycle of encouragement*. If you set reasonable standards which can be achieved, the results offer you the opportunity to say 'well done', and this encourages everyone to do better. In this way, the cycle reinforces itself. Unfortunately there is also a negative cycle which is easy to get into: you have expectations which cannot be met, and you express dissatisfaction at the result; the person is discouraged, they perform less well, and you become even more critical. Always use a positive cycle of encouragement.

One of the most powerful ways of setting up a positive cycle is by target setting, which was discussed in Chapter 4, and consultation (Chapter 3).

We can express the link between effort and results by the statement:

$$method \times effort = results$$

Results may not be achieved because of unreasonably high expectations, lack of effort, poor work method, or a combination of these factors. Poor results discourage and demotivate staff.

Good target setting predicts attainable results, and consultation allows for modified methods. This combination dramatically changes the equation to:

$$\frac{Their}{method} \times \frac{committed}{effort} = \frac{achieved}{targets} + \frac{motivated}{staff}$$

Remember how much effort we all put into proving our own methods and how hard we work to achieve targets we have agreed. Use this knowledge to get better results.

People: the vital resource

Results are what you are judged on, and they depend on more than target settings and consultations. People are the vital resource you use to get results.

Concentrate on *communication*; make it clear, concise and acceptable. Take care with your objectives; be thorough with your instructions and considerate when allocating work. Try not to assume too much. In general we recommend the 'theory Y' style of supervision.

Self-check

How would you describe the 'theory Y' style of supervision? (Two minutes.)

'Theory Y' describes the belief that people are honest, enjoy their work and accept responsibility. The explanation of this is outlined in Chapter 3. 'Theory Y' does not mean being soft and indecisive; it means being straight, consulting people, setting a good example and leading your team. If you know where you are going and what your objectives are, you can impart that *feeling of direction* to your staff.

If problems crop up, and you have to give orders, try to depersonalise the situation. Do not say, 'I am telling what to do', but use the logic of the situation and say, 'The situation is this and it requires that action; therefore I am asking you to do it'. Let the *force of the situation* make the demand.

Roles affect behaviour

Another factor to remember is that the role people perceive they are in determines the *way they behave*. A person who is treated as a responsible adult will act like one and the roles of worker and responsible adult can easily be combined.

Your staff have many roles. They are at work for only a part of their life. They leave their work role at work and take on their family role. Members of your staff at home will see themselves differently how they perceive themselves in their work roles.

In organisations the concept of role extends into the link between jobs in the organisation (the idea of role relationships is explored in Chapter 8. This is important because there are two sets of relationships:

relationships *between people*, whether Fred gets on with Joe; and relationships *between the roles that they are in*. Does the role of supervisor match the role of inspector (or auditor)? If there is a mismatch of roles, it will create conflict between the people, even if they get on well as individuals. Organisations set up roles which sometimes cannot help but conflict. If you spot this situation, try to get the parties concerned to see the real situation.

9.3 Learn to Manage the Boss

As a supervisor you are a front line manager, part of the management team. You are the link between your manager and the people in your section. Do not be put off if your manager pressures you; no doubt he (or she) is also under pressure. Keep the work going but keep part of your mind alert as the observer of the section, even if you are involved in a technical or a work problem. Discuss your objectives with your manager. Keep a balanced view, so that you can present the boss with your arguments and suggestions in a positive form – this will help you grow in the job. And don't forget that you are also in partnership with your team, who also need to know your objectives.

Answers to Exercises

Exercise 2.1
Subordinate S3 is now responsible for carrying out the task X. But that is not the end of the matter, because the manager still has some responsibility. The distinction is that S3 has the responsibility for doing task X, but the manager has the responsibility for making sure that the task is completed properly. He is *accountable* for the results of S3's work.

Exercise 2.2
These may have been some of the elements common to all supervisory work that you listed:

- The supervisor has to *organise the work* of the people in his section.
- The supervisor is responsible for *achieving the required results* in the *most effective way*.
- The supervisor is in *direct contact* with *those who do the work*.
- The supervisor is the *first person* to hear about any *problems* that may occur.
- The supervisor has to *create the climate* in the section and *exercise control and immediate discipline*.
- The supervisor's managerial freedom is often *restricted by the organisation*:

  – the work is planned by specialists;
  – budgets are agreed and controlled by the manager;
  – in large firms methods are tightly defined;
  – the supervisor always has to work within company procedures.

Exercise 2.3
These are some of the differences you should have spotted:

- The *time span* of each job.
- The *consequences of delay/failure*.
- The *number of jobs in work* at any one time.
- The *variety of jobs*.
- The *variety of trades/skills* needed.

Exercise 3.1

The three components of attitude are:

- Predisposition to action.
- Knowledge.
- Feelings

While these three elements are the fundamental constituents of attitude, there is no easy, or quick way to *change anyone's attitude*.

Exercise 3.2

1 Physiological needs, safety needs, social needs, esteem needs, self-actualisation needs.
2 'Theory Y'.
3 The danger most people see is that of being taken advantage of. People will think you are weak if you use 'theory Y'.

How well did you answer these questions?
Did you remember the stages in Maslow's hierarchy?
How about Question 2? I have assumed that you would prefer a 'Y-type' manager – was I right?
Have you been 'ripped off' when you used a 'Y' approach?

Exercise 3.3

Your answer may vary from ours, but here are some ideas:

- Try to sort out *complaints* from *symptoms*.
- Check *your own* perception and objectives.
- Tell them how *you* feel.
- Ask for *information* and *suggestions*.
- Go for a *win–win* result.
- Contain the problems *within the group* for as long as you can.
- Do not *curry favour*.

Exercise 4.1

Statement 1 is planning: Tom is looking ahead and rescheduling the work of his section.
Statement 2 is allocating work, so it is part of the organising stage.
Statement 3 is checking up on the progress of the work, part of controlling.

Statement **4** indicates that Tom is getting involved in the doing, although it is mixed with some organising.

Statement **5** is also organising, with some explanation as to the urgency of the work.

Exercise 4.2
The most important questions would be:

- What sort of dance should it be? A low cost knees-up or a posh, upmarket affair?
- What will we set for the price of a ticket?
- Where should it be held? Is the hall available?
- What time of the season should we hold it?
- What sort of band do we want? What bands are available?
- How shall we organise the publicity?
- Will we make a profit? Will it meet our objectives?

Exercise 4.3
The choices open to Dave are:

- Put one person in a room and make it his or her responsibility.
- Work the group as a gang and keep them together, moving from room to room with him as overseer.
- Split into pairs and work the rooms in succession.
- Let the three specialise, some cleaning down, some painting.

The factors to be considered are:

- The *expertise* in the group; for example, is any of the three skilful as a painter?
- The *equipment* available. Will there be enough trestles for four people to work separately?
- The set-up which is most likely to encourage a good *performance*. Will the group be self-motivating?
- The *available space*. With four in a room, will they get in each other's way?
- The benefits of specialising. If a person sticks to doing one particular job, will he become *more expert* at it?

Exercise 4.4
Remember that the control requires *five* elements. These are listed with the parts of the supervisor's statement that show that control is being operated here:

'I see that Judith is wearing terrible stockings again' – *measurement* of Judith's performance and *comparisons* with *standard*.

'. . . they do not conform to company rules' – *standard* expressed in the *company rules*.

'I shall have to speak to her' – *feedback of the variance* to Judith.

' . . . and get her to change them' – *corrective action* that the supervisor has pulled Judith back into line.

Exercise 4.5

Allocated work – this is central to his work as a supervisor.

Dealt with a technical problem – this is doubtful: it is outside his responsibilities but may have been necessary to keep the work flowing. There is a danger that Ian may have allowed himself to be drawn into this because he is interested in it.

Discussed with Production Control – this is responsibility 3: form and planning.

Helped the Supervisor in the stores – this is not central to his responsibilities but time invested into building relationships with people who can help you is never wasted.

Showed a trainee – this is responsibility 4: training, so it is very important.

Exercise 5.1

Here are some of the many details that you could have listed:

- Age.
- Intelligence.
- Level of knowledge.
- Attitudes.
- Frame of mind.
- History/background.

Exercise 5.2

Here are some samples for you to consider:

- 'George, that floor's looking a bit grubby; give it a quick once-over.'
- 'George, sweep that floor.'
- 'George, sweep that floor now.'
- 'George, drop everything and clean that xxxx floor *now*.'
- 'Oi, you – yes, you – get that floor swept now.'

Exercise 5.3

Did you remember *all* the steps we examined? Here is the list again.

The communication process

- Step 1 The objective: What do I want to happen?
- Step 2 The Sender: How does the sender of a message influence the message?
- Step 3 The receiver: Is there anything I need to know about the person who receives my message?
- Step 4 Barriers: Is there anything that could prevent my message getting through?
- Step 5 The medium: How should I pass this message? Chat, memo, telephone, letter?
- Step 6 The tone style: Should I be formal? Casual?
- Step 7 The message: What do I put in, leave out?
- Step 8 Control: Does the message say what I want it to? Will it get the desired result?
- Step 9 Transmit: Send the message.
- Step 10 Feedback: Has my message been (1) received, (2) understood (3) accepted?
- Step 11 Modification: How easily can I modify the message?

Which step(s) are you good at?
Which step(s) needs working on?

Exercise 5.4
- Oral communication is used because it is *less formal* than written communication.
- It is *more flexible* (you can say things that you cannot write!)
- It is easy to change to *suit the receiver*.
- You get *instant feedback*.
- It is *quick*.
- Some people find it *easier* than the written equivalent, etc.

There are, however, disadvantages with oral communication:

- There is *no record* to refer to.
- There may be *misunderstandings*, especially if oral messages are passed on.
- It can consume *lots of time* if many people are to be told.
- In noisy places it can be *difficult*, and *misunderstood*.

The general communication skills will obviously still apply.

Exercise 6.1

Example 1

- Control information: assistant – restock level; manager – sales rate and ratios.
- Operating information: assistant – price of product.

Example 2

- Control information: machinist – some data will govern *how* he makes the parts – i.e., data that controls finish, accuracy; the finish time controls his work rate; supervisor – information on parts holding up assembly can be used to control priorities, as can material availability control job priority; some manufacturing data will control the choice of machine required and the machinist selected.
- Operating information: machinist – some manufacturing data, start time; supervisor – all his information is also operating information.

Exercise 6.2

You probably had most of the following:

- Giving work instructions.
- Training staff.
- Meetings.
- Interviewing.
- Writing memos, letters, reports and notices.
- Passing information to others.
- Collecting information.

To do these effectively, you have to apply the *process of communication*. Use this list to decide which applications you need to concentrate on.

Exercise 6.3

Your answer will depend on whether the instruction you considered was to make an item or to give a service. Here is a possible list:

- The person being instructed.
- The task itself.
- The match of task and person selected.
- Time.
- The instruction method, medium, language barriers.
- The supervisor's skills at communication.

- The procedure to follow in doing the task.
- The resources needed.
- The standards to be achieved.

We consider that the most important factor is the *person receiving the instruction*.

Exercise 6.4

1 You may have listed one or all of the following: member; representative; specialist; organiser.
2 You are an individual; only you know how you perceive meetings. (See Chapter 3 for 'perception', if you are unfamiliar with the term.) Generally the more involved you are in the meeting the more affected you are by the outcome and conduct of the meeting.

Your feelings will depend on the *result of the meeting* and your *own interests*.

Exercise 6.5

We hope you automatically listed all the skills of oral communication for both 1 and 2. You should have listed some or all of the following:

1 Depending on whether you are a member, representative or a specialist, these are: *listening* – all groups; *persuading* – varies with role; *steering* – varies with role; *summarising* for understanding.
2 The chairperson needs all those above, and more. Here are some skills the chairperson needs: planning; analytical skills for setting objectives and ordering subjects on agenda; organising; to be able to look after minority interests and control people; be firm and fair; be sensitive to people's feelings; to react quickly to change.

Exercise 6.6

The answer to the first question should be 'yes'. Coaching involves:

- Listening.
- Summarising.
- Letting the problem owner restate the problem.
- Encouraging the problem owner to solve their own problems.
- Not imposing your solution.

The steps do not necessarily occur in this order, as they vary from problem to problem. Often you have to give information to the problem owner. Sometimes the problem is restated more than once.

Exercise 7.1

The calculations are:

1 $(5 \div 100) \times 450 = 22.5$, a rise of £22.50 per month. New pay = £472.50.

2 Increase is $3,250 - 2,850 = 400$. $(400 \div 2,850) \times 100 = 14\%$ increase.

3 The works cost of £3.75 represents 108%. The previous works cost was $(100 \div 108) \times 3.75 = £3.47$.

Exercise 7.2

1 The proportion of women is $\frac{3}{5}$ of the whole. $\frac{3}{5} \times 15 = 9$ women. There are therefore 6 men.

2 The ratio of photographic to audio sales is 6,000 : 4,500. The simplest figure that state this are 4 : 3. The proportion of total sales earned by audio is $\frac{3}{7}$. As a percentage this is $(3 \div 7) \times 100 = 42.8\%$.

3 Total number of people employed is $50 + 30 + 70 = 150$.

Proportion of people in department X is $50 \div 150 = \frac{3}{3}$. Cost allocated to dept X is $(50 \div 150) \times 3,000 = £1,000$.

Similarly dept Y is $(30 \div 150) \times 3,000 = £600$, and dept Z is $(70 \ 150) \times 3,000 = £1,400$.

Exercise 7.3

Arithmetic mean = (total of all the ages $\div$ number of people) = $499 \div 12 = 41.6$ years.

If we rank the ages in order, 18,23,36,38,44, 46,46 46,48,48,52,54, the median value is 46 years.

The mode is also 46 years.

The diagram is as in Figure A1.1.

Exercise 7.4

Taxes and savings: $32 \div 160 \times 360 = 72°$. Entertainment is the same, $72°$.

Rent: $(24 \div 160) \times 360 = 54°$.

Clothes: $(16 \div 160) \times 360 = 36°$.

The total of angles should of course add up to 360°. The completed pie chart will look as in Figure A1.2, and should be neatly labelled so that each portion of the pie is clearly identified. You must decide whether it is best to write the labels on the circle or use lines from the label to the appropriate sector.

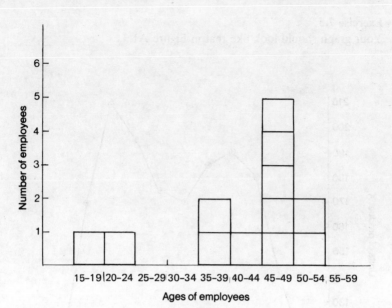

Fig A1.1   *Brackets Ltd: age distribution (Exercise 7.3)*

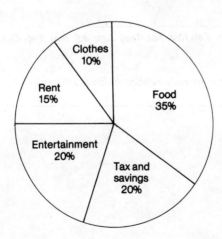

Fig A1.2   *Pie chart: allocation of average family expenditure (Exercise 7.4)*

214 *Answers to Exercises*

Exercise 7.5
Your graph should look like that in Figure A1.3.

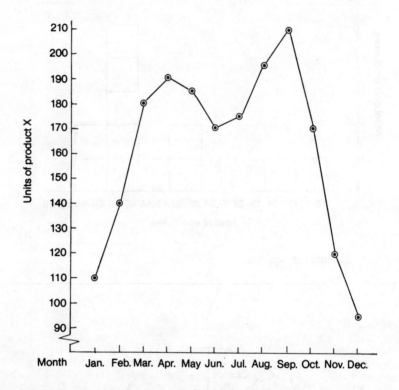

Fig A1.3   *Product X: monthly variation in demand (Exercise 7.5)*

Exercise 7.6
Your flow process chart should look like that in Figure A1.4.

FLOW PROCESS CHART		PERSON TYPE *(Secretary)*
OPERATION: *Preparation of letter*		
DISTANCE (metres)	SYMBOL	DESCRIPTION
	①	*Receives call from manager*
	①▷	*To manager's office*
	②	*Take shorthand notes as manager dictates*
	◁②	*To secretary's office*
	③	*When ready, type letter*
	③▷	*When batch of letters is complete, to manager's office*
	①	*Wait while manager checks letter*
	◁④	*To secretary's office*
	④	*Prepare letter for posting*

Fig A1.4   *Flow process chart: preparation of a letter (Exercise 7.6)*

Exercise 7.7
The best charting methods would be:

1 A combination of flow process for the sequence and flow diagrams for the movements.
2 'Sequence' is the key word here, indicating a flow process chart.
3 A multiple activity chart to show how their actions interrelate.
4 Here again the flow process chart for sequence and the flow diagram for movement.

Exercise 7.8

Putting these actual times in the formula comparing them against a standard time of 0.85 standard hours, we get performances of 106, 71, 89, 118.

Check these against the rating scale to see what the numbers signify.

Exercise 7.9

Your Gantt chart should look like that in Figure A1.5a.

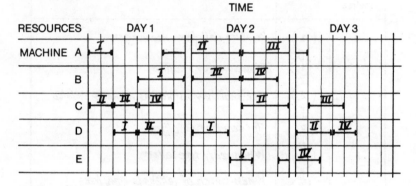

Loaded in sequence I, II, III, IV. Completed by the end of the 5th hour on Day 3.

Fig A1.5a *Gantt chart: work loading batches I, II, III and IV*

Exercise 7.10

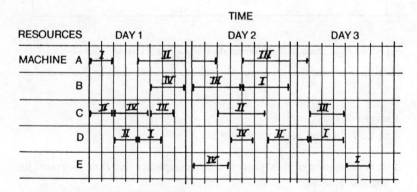

Loaded in sequence II, IV, III, I. No! It is not a quicker way, the time needed is extended by one hour.

Fig A1.5b *Gantt chart: work loading, batch II loaded first*

Exercise 8.1

There are three key points where the people involved went wrong:

- Janet and her boss left the section to run itself, apparently without nominating a deputy section leader, so that Liz had to make her own decision about doing the trial for Mark.
- Mark overstepped his authority in pressing Liz to do the trial and put her routine work aside.
- When Mark first appeared on the scene to start the implementation, Janet and her boss should have agreed with Mark and his boss just how far Mark could go in order to get the trials done.

Your diagram should look like that in Figure A1.6.

Exercise 8.2

By drawing a vertical line at the 140 point we can see that revenue exceeds total cost by £260; this is the profit. By calculation we know that the revenue will be 140 × £5 = £700. The total cost will be made up of

---

Fig A1.6   *Janet, Mark and Janet's boss: section structure (Exercise 8.1)*

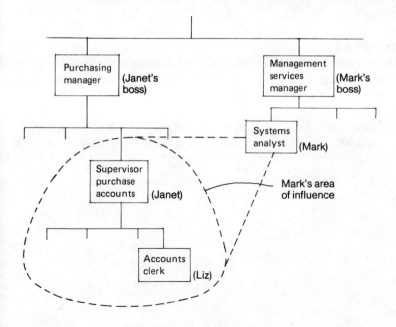

the fixed cost which is £160 and the variable cost which will be 140 × £2 = £280, so total cost is £440. Therefore, the profit by calculation at a sale of 140 tickets will be £700 *less* £440, which is £260.

Exercise 8.3
- At 70 tickets sold, the unit cost is (160 + 140) ÷70 = £4.30.
- At 110 tickets sold, the unit cost is (160 + 220) ÷ 110 = £3.45.
- At 150 tickets sold, the unit cost is (160 + 300) ÷ 150 = £3.10.

Exercise 8.4
The five elements of a control system were outlined in Chapter 4, and we listed them there as:

- A *standard or plan* which the control seeks to maintain.
- Measurement of the *actual achievement*.
- Comparison of the *actual against the standard*.
- Feedback of any *variances* detected at the comparison.
- Corrective action to *bring the system under control*.

Exercise 8.5
Material costs will be:

Jan.	Feb.	Mar.	Apr.	May	Jun.
£3,000	£4,200	£5,000	£6,000	£6,000	£5,600

Exercise 8.6
The revenue for February will be from January's production of 150 chairs, making a total of 150 × £25 = £3,750. Similarly for the other months, giving a revenue table like this:

Jan.	Feb.	Mar.	Apr.	May	Jun.
£10,000	£6,750	£9,450	£11,250	£13,500	£13,500

Index